Testing People
A Practical Guide
to Psychometrics

NFER-NELSON ASSESSMENT LIBRARY

Testing People
A Practical Guide to Psychometrics

Edited by
John R Beech and Leonora Harding

Published by The NFER-NELSON Publishing Company Ltd.,
Darville House, 2 Oxford Road East,
Windsor, Berkshire SL4 1DF, England.

First published 1990
© 1990, John R. Beech and Leonora Harding

British Library Cataloguing in Publication Data
Testing people : a practical guide to psychometrics. – (The
   NFER-NELSON assessment library).
   I. Psychometrics
   I. Beech, John R.   II. Harding, Leonora 1944–
   152.8

ISBN 0-7005-1255-1
ISBN 0-7005-1256-X pbk

Printed by Billing & Sons Ltd, Worcester
Phototypeset by David John Services Ltd., Maidenhead

Softback :
ISBN 0 7005 1256 X
Code 8502 02 4

Hardback :
ISBN 0 7005 1255 1
Code 8501 02 4

Contents

List of Boxes and Figures

List of Contributors

David Bartram is Reader in Psychology at the University of Hull.
Chris French is Lecturer in Psychology at Goldsmiths College, University of London.
Paul Kline is Professor of Psychology at the University of Exeter.
Tim Pring is Lecturer in Speech Therapy at the City University, London.

Series Editors' Preface

The word 'assessment' conjures an adverse emotional reaction in many people. We have all, at some stage, undergone an assessment in some form – for instance when sitting an examination – and many of us have found it a distinctly unpleasant experience. Why should we make assessments of people, and even more to the point, why launch a series of volumes on the subject?

Assessment is usually to do with making a judgement about an individual in relation to a large group of people, based on the acquisition of a body of knowledge concerning that individual. In carrying out an assessment the professional believes that it is necessary to make such an assessment as a basis for deciding a particular course of action. This activity is considered to be predominantly in the best interests of the person being assessed; at times, it will also protect the interests of society, or an organization, such as a company. Whether or not one agrees with the concept of making an assessment, the practice continues in our society, even if it waxes and wanes in some professional sectors. Our own view is that assessment is here to stay and in many cases is beneficial to the individual.

It is important that the best available means of assessment are used by professional workers to provide an accurate body of knowledge on which to base decisions. Errors of diagnosis can sometimes have serious consequences. The national press seems to report almost every day on situations in which diagnosis has been problematic, such as releasing a violent prisoner prematurely, or making erroneous accusations of child abuse, and so on. Less dramatic situations are sometimes described in which a child is inaccurately assessed and is then put on a training programme which is not appropriate for his or her needs, or where an elderly person is inaccurately considered as unable to live in his or her own home and transferred to another environment. Given that many of these assessments are essential, improving their accuracy is a worthwhile goal. If this series of volumes is instrumental in improving accuracy to some degree, we shall be well pleased.

As well as inaccurate use of tests, breakdown of communication between professions can lead to wrong decisions and inappropriate therapy or placement plans. Any one client may be treated, assessed or discussed by a number of professionals with different training, areas of expertise or approaches to assessment and vocabulary. (The term 'client' itself suggests one particular approach to care.) This series is explicitly directed to the sharing of knowledge and to the breaking down of barriers between professionals. We believe multidisciplinary cooperation and information exchange can only benefit the subjects of assessment. It should be borne in mind, however, that certain tests which have been reviewed in these volumes can only be applied by professionals with the appropriate qualifications. We hope that there will be a certain amount of liberalization of these strictures in the future in order to facilitate cooperation between professionals.

When planning the series we decided early on that we were not going to produce exhaustive manuals, giving thorough reviews of all possible assessment techniques. There are many books of this nature already available. We thought that it would be a much better idea to produce fairly short books aimed at a particular category of person requiring assessment, such as the elderly, or those with speech and language difficulties. Our readership would be the professional workers involved with such groups, either directly as assessors or indirectly as those who use test results in their decision making. Students training for these professions, or professionals undergoing in-service training will also find these useful. Therefore, we set our writers a very difficult task. Each contribution had to be easy to read, but at the same time, provide information that the current professional worker would find useful when deciding on an assessment strategy. The writer might point to a new test that has been developed, or highlight the inadequacies of one currently used. The chapters do describe the application of tests within a particular area, but they also provide a range of other useful information, for instance, check lists, case studies, points to bear in mind with certain types of patient, and so on.

Most of the volumes contain a final section of reviews on the main tests currently applied in that area. Making choices about what to include has been difficult; but the final choice is based on extensive consultation with practising professionals and researchers. The end result should contain the tests used most frequently within an area. The problem is that there is usually a large variety of more minor tests, each of which is probably used by only a few workers. From this group we have chosen those tests that seem to contain a feature or application of outstanding interest, or those tests that we felt deserved wider use.

All of the test reviews are written within a pre-arranged structure. Information is given about the purpose of the test, how to use it and an evaluation is also made. Some technical information is provided, such as the number of people who were tested in order to develop the test. Where available, the reliability and validity are supplied. The reliability shows the extent-to which applying the same test again will give the same result. A low reliability indicates that assessment could be inaccurate as the outcome changes on successive occasions. The validity of the test shows how well the test is associated with similar tests measuring the same properties. The reader does not necessarily need any prior knowledge in order to understand these test reviews. However, the present book on psychometrics is for the interested reader who wishes to go into the statistical basis of testing in more depth. This is a corner-stone volume in the series, designed for professional people who wish to update their statistical knowledge in order to understand the basis of the tests. It does not assume any previous statistical knowledge.

Preface

The book begins with an introduction to the main issues in testing and then begins by giving extensive coverage to the important concept of correlation. This part of the text, in particular, is accompanied by illustrative figures and worked examples so that the reader can gain a firm understanding of the necessary concepts. This is followed by a detailed examination of the concepts of reliability and validity which have already been briefly described. The next part of the book goes into the practical details of test construction, and then gives advice on how to evaluate tests and how these are best suited to one's needs. The volume continues in the same pragmatic vein by examining the case-study approach to assessment. Psychometric tests are based on large populations, but how can one assess an individual who displays a set of problems not likely to be present in the same configuration in other people? The final chapter of the book examines the developing field of computer-assisted assessment, indicating potential problems that need to be monitored as well as the potential advantages of this approach.

In summary, the book assumes no basic statistical knowledge but enables any professional worker to build up their knowledge on the statistical basis of assessment, to produce their own assessment tests and to learn about other forms of assessing people.

Finally, we would like to thank Ian Florance and Diana Hilton-Jones of NFER-NELSON for their enthusiasm and close involvement with the series from its inception as well as the numerous other individuals who have given their help.

JOHN R. BEECH and LEONORA HARDING

Introduction

David Bartram

Testing and assessment goes on all the time: it seems that no-one escapes! Most people are assessed at some time in their lives: for career guidance, job selection, speech and language development as children; to check whether, as babies, they are developing normally or, towards the end of their lives, how well they can cope with the demands of their houses or flats. Assessment may take place in school, at a recruitment consultancy, at home, at a speech therapy clinic – even in a car. Many people believe the driving test to be the most stressful assessment of all! Assessments may be carried out by a psychologist, a teacher, a doctor or a personnel manager, and may take any number of forms – questionnaires, gazing at ink blots, matching two designs, operating a computer keyboard or replicating real-life working tasks. Assessment may even – in its loosest sense – take the form of a professionally qualified person watching an event, recording its crucial features, analysing them and then deciding on a course of action.

Finally, and most importantly, assessment will lead to some sort of action: promotion of a member of staff, the commitment of a client to sheltered accommodation, the construction and implementation of a particular course of treatment. Some assessments (perhaps too many) may only result in the decision to publish a research paper! In the context of this book, it is crucial to keep in mind that assessment should be *purposive* rather than, as so often seems the case, *self-validating*. One assesses in order to decide on a course of action, rather than for the joy of testing itself. I shall return to this point below.

The NFER-NELSON Assessment Library series, of which this book is a part, touches on many – but not all – of these forms of assessment, as they are used in industry, social and health-related services and education. This volume concentrates on the statistical basis of testing. As the techniques described here have mainly been developed by psychologists, these are usually referred to as psychometric techniques. However, we shall normally eschew this term and use the more neutral expression: 'the statistical basis of testing' as an indication that these techniques for test construction can be used widely in the general context of assessment. If the rest of the series is about the methods and actual assessments applied within specific areas, this book looks at some of the techniques and issues underlying many of these tests.

While most psychologists will have some understanding of and experience in these techniques, it is important at this stage to give other professions a brief introduction to the area, and to show that these statistical techniques may be – and are being – used by a wide variety of professionals, for many different purposes.

Psychometrics is the branch of psychology concerned with the measurement of mental processes such as intelligence, fear, anxiety, extroversion and logical thinking. In practice, such processes cannot be measured directly as they are not observable: they are hypothetical constructs. You cannot measure anxiety in the same way you can measure your hat size.

However, there are many things about people that can be measured, from physiological processes (such as rate of heart beat) to actual behaviours (for instance how quickly a person can press a button when a light comes on, or how many answers he or she gives correctly in a test of reading). We can also measure what people say about their own behaviours and mental states (by asking questions such as 'Are you feeling anxious?' or 'Do you drink too much?' and grading the answers). This observable behaviour provides the raw material from which psychologists draw conclusions about an individual's mental processes, states and traits; his or her ability to succeed at a particular job or the specific causes of notably aberrant behaviour. However, to extrapolate from observable behaviour back to underlying processes needs great care and a complex system of checks to ensure that unwarranted conclusions are not drawn. The statistical techniques described in this book provide just such a system of checks.

Statistically-based tests are distinguished from other forms of assessment by the fact that they produce numerical scores. These 'raw' scores (the basic measurements taken or scores achieved) are then manipulated using statistical techniques – many of which are described in this book – and can then be compared with normative data or examined for certain meaningful properties.

Why Should We Bother About Statistically-based Assessment?

While they were developed as part of the discipline of psychology, these techniques can be applied to many other professional needs. Look through this book briefly, and you may wonder if it is worth making the effort. Using these techniques may require you to understand a number of statistical techniques, with which you may have no familiarity; to find out about enormous numbers of tests, before administering one and finding out information that you can already gather, using experience and professional judgement in perhaps half the time. For instance some case workers may feel they do not need a test to tell them when an elderly person needs sheltered accommodation; experienced personnel managers may believe they can spot a born salesperson as he or she walks through the door (or at least after they have read their application form and asked a few questions). It is worth pointing out that statistically-based assessment provides a counterbalance to understandably over-confident, subjective decision-making.

It is true that there are drawbacks and limitations to statistically-based testing. It is not applicable to every situation, nor do practical considerations and time constraints make it appropriate in others. The techniques can, at first, seem complex, though they are based on fairly simple statistical concepts. Test users, unlike test constructors, do not need to become psychometricians – they only need to gain sufficient understanding of the techniques to use the test properly. Finally, these tests must always be used in association with other sources of information – your experience, professional knowledge and documentation (case notes, reports, CVs, etc.).

The major advantage of statistically-based assessment – and it is crucial to professional effectiveness and quality of decision-making – is that it provides an objective source of data, unbiased by subjective feelings. We place too much weight on subjective evidence in our decision-making: research has shown over and over again that even the most stringent interview, the most careful application of training, the most detailed study of reports will lead to errors. Most people know of the syndrome (known as the 'Halo Effect') by which interviewers tend to choose candidates they like or who are like themselves, unconsciously rationalizing that they will be good at the job. This sort of 'hidden subjectivity' affects many of our judgements. Decisions made without objective information can have damaging, even shattering, implications for the clients of health departments, social services and schools. Without the ability to justify objectively such decisions, they can also have deleterious effects on the professionals involved, as recent suspected child abuse cases have shown.

As I have mentioned, we put too much weight on our subjective judgements. Not only do the techniques described in this book provide objective data, they *also provide a measure of how much reliance we can put on those data*, by giving us quantifiable levels of confidence relating to our statements about people. No measurement is perfectly accurate (see Chapter 2) but is accurate within certain error margins. The lower the error margin, the more confidence we can place in the measure; the higher the error margin, the more we need to think about whether we are addressing the right problem, whether we need to delay a decision and search for further confirmation or refutation of our ideas.

Thus we should be enabled to make better decisions, based on an awareness of the limitations of the data we gather. This is above all about creating measures that, under certain conditions, measure what they claim to measure and which only make claims that can be justified. The technical terms 'reliability' and 'validity' are central to these issues, and form the subject matter of Chapter 3.

It can be seen from the above discussion that statistically-based tests are like icebergs: the largest and most significant parts are beneath the surface. A fun newspaper questionnaire and a psychometric test might have exactly the same questions or items ('Do you feel tired most of the time?' for instance). What distinguishes one from the other is not the surface contents but the underlying body of information allied to statistics about people's responses to the test's content. The way in which you decide whether an assessment tool is statistically-based or not is by examining its documentation.

THE TEST MANUAL

A test manual should contain all the information needed in order to assess the test's psychometric properties, its relevance for your particular purposes, how to administer and score it and what to do with the scores once you have got them. One of the purposes of this book – made explicit in

Paul Kline's Chapter 5 'Selecting the Best Test' – is to enable you to find this information and evaluate it, by raising some of the issues that will enable you to decide whether a test is relevant to your needs.

A good manual will contain a lot of technical information about the test. Some users are put off by this, and are tempted simply to read through the administration and scoring procedures before using a test. Tests used in this way are worse than useless, for they can cause actual harm to the person being assessed by providing incorrect information which, none the less, is presented in a spuriously precise, numerical form.

If you want to decide whether a test is relevant to your client's problem and then use the resulting data responsibly, it is important to read through the manual, understand the rationale underlying its construction (see Chapter 4) and examine the data that define its reliability, validity and the distributional characteristics of its scores (see Chapters 2 and 3 where these terms are fully explained). This book will give you the basic information you need to understand most of the data presented in test manuals.

It must be remembered, particularly when reading Chapter 4, that you, as a test *user*, do not have to master all the statistical techniques required of a test *constructor*. This book gives a selection of these techniques but there are many more complex ways of constructing tests and manipulating data, described in other advanced books. What is important is that you learn to understand what the data reported in the manual mean – what the data imply about the test's purposes; its underlying concepts; the stringency of its construction; the amount of trust you can put in its results, and to whom you can reliably administer it.

While Chapters 2, 3, 4 and 5 go into these data in some detail, Box 1.1 gives you an indication of the sort of information you might find in a test manual. The *Graduate and Managerial Assessment* (Blinkhorn, 1985) is used to select graduates for employment in industry and to plan promotion of staff to managerial positions. It contains three 'high level' tests of ability (Numerical, Verbal and Abstract reasoning). Part 1 of the *GMA* manual provides a detailed description of the rationale underlying the construction of each test; how and in what sort of situations one might use it; how the items and the format of the tests were developed; and how the initial psychometric trials were carried out.

Part 2 provides essential practical guidance on how to administer and score the test. While this is extremely important, it is perhaps the 'easiest' part of the manual to deal with. Part 3 then deals with interpretation. Typically, this section of a manual will discuss the interpretation of 'raw scores' (*i.e.* the actual numbers obtained from scoring the test) and the conversion of raw scores to percentile or standard scores (see Chapter 2) through the use of norm tables. Central to understanding these procedures is a good grasp of some basic statistical concepts: including the *mean, standard deviation, variance and standard error*. All these will be explained in detail in Chapter 2.

The 'interpretation' section of the manual will also present evidence for the reliability and validity of the test. As has been mentioned before, these two issues lie at the centre of test interpretation and are of crucial importance. The whole of Chapter 3 is devoted to reliability and validity and you will find their importance stressed in subsequent chapters (especially Chapters 4 and 5). Briefly, the reliability data tell you how much reliance you can place upon a score – how 'accurate' it is – while the validity data tend to focus on two main areas: how confident you can be that the test is measuring what is purports to measure, and what sort of inferences you can reasonably draw from the person's scores.

Much of the information on reliability and validity in test manuals is presented in the form of *correlation coefficients*, with the reliability data being used to compute the *standard error of measurement* for each scale. Both of these statistics are described in detail in the following two chapters.

The final section of the GMA manual (Box 1.1) contains technical data. This is essential reference material (and for many tests will form the bulk of the manual). Included in this section should be norm tables (which you use to convert raw scores to other forms of measure); statistical information about each of the items in the test; breakdowns of data on various different samples of people; and summaries of the results of relevant validation studies.

For some tests, there is so much data available that it is not practical to put it all in one manual. For example, the *Cattell Sixteen Personality Factor Questionnaire* (16PF) – a personality test used widely by psychologists and personnel staff in industry – has a large technical handbook which contains a wealth of information about the test's development and interpretation. There are a large number of different normative supplements, containing tables for converting raw scores to standard scores for all sorts of different groups from various different countries. There is an administrator's manual – that concentrates mainly on the procedures of administration and scoring – and there are a number of interpretative guides (e.g. Karson and O'Dell, 1976; Krug, 1981). In addition to all these there is a massive scientific literature describing research studies using the 16PF.

The mere presence of all this information does not imply that the test is either a 'good' one or a 'bad' one. But it does mean that information exists from which one can judge the appropriateness of a test for a particular purpose.

Anyone who uses the test should absorb enough of this information to appreciate both its strengths and its limitations. Interpreting personality profiles from tests like the 16PF requires a great deal of study and experience. A firm grounding in the statistical basis of testing covered in Chapters 2 and 3, will help to build your understanding of the more *qualitative* aspects of test interpretation.

STEPS IN THE ASSESSMENT PROCESS

It may help to reinforce the importance of a thorough knowledge of the literature that accompanies a test if we look at the steps involved in actually carrying out an assessment. The assessment process consists of seven main steps:
1. Test selection
2. Administration
3. Scoring
4. Analysis of test measures
5. Interpretation of test measures
6. Client feedback
7. Decision-making

Box 1.1

Outline of contents of the GMA manual

Part 1: The tests
 Introduction
 Numerical
   Rationale
   Application
   Development
   Pilot studies and standardization
 Verbal
   Rationale
   Application
   Development
   Pilot studies and standardization
 Abstract
   Rationale
   Application
   Development
   Pilot studies and standardization
Part 2: Administration and scoring
 Administration
 Scoring instructions
Part 3: Interpretation
 Interpreting scores
   Norm tables
   Standardization sample
   Raw scores
   Standard scores
   Parallelism
   Analysis of standardization data
 Reliability
   The speed factor
   Local independence
   Internal consistency of GMA–A
 Differences among individuals
 Combining scores
 Validity
   Numerical
   Verbal
   Abstract
 Correlations amongst GMA tests
Part 4: Technical information
 Norm tables and standard score conversion
 Item analyses
 Sub-sample information
 Validation studies
References

The relative importance of each of these steps depends very much on the nature and function of the assessment. For example, in vocational counselling, the 'decision-making' component is far less important than client feedback, while the opposite tends to be the case in occupational selection.

Choosing which test (or tests) to use for a given purpose requires a high level of knowledge about the nature of available tests, their statistical properties and their usefulness for a particular client population. You need to be able to make judgements about the relative appropriateness of each of a number of alternative tests. To do this you require sufficient knowledge to be able to evaluate the information presented in each test manual – or indeed to notice when important information is missing from the manual.

Actual test administration can be broken down into a number of substages.

1. Presentation of instructions
2. Administration of example and test items
3. Collection and recording of subjects' responses

The level of expertise required for test administration varies considerably from one test to another. However, in all those cases where test administration can be separated from interpretation, the expertise required is essentially procedural: that is, you may need training in how to administer a test, but do not need a knowledge of psychometrics. As test administration is frequently a standardized, somewhat mechanical procedure, it is the assessment step that has been most often automated (see Chapter 7).

Like administration, scoring tends – for most tests – to be a mechanical process that could readily be automated. However, some forms of assessment, particularly the more *projective* ones (such as the famous *Rorschach Ink Blot Test*), often rely on the scorer making judgements. For different scorers to produce reliable measures from such tests, the scoring rules need to be as specific as possible, and the judges need to be highly skilled and experienced.

Analysis of test scores can be distinguished from interpretation in that analysis involves the manipulation of raw scores to provide other useful statistics; interpretation involves saying what those statistics mean. Analysis can range from simple procedures like using norm tables, to more complex ones like computing various forms of prediction equation. Test interpretation involves 'going beyond' the analysis and saying what the measures mean.

In order to interpret a test, a good knowledge of the test and its validity is required, plus the knowledge and experience necessary to draw valid conclusions from the results. Analysis and interpretation both require a detailed in-depth knowledge of the test manual and any other relevant supporting documentation.

The ability to provide feedback to clients requires more than just skill in test interpretation. It also requires the ability to communicate a valid interpretation of the test results in terms comprehensible and appropriate to the 'lay' client, and, depending upon the situation, some degree of counselling skill.

Finally, assessment data are used to aid the making of decisions. Should we hire this person? Who should we promote? What advice can we offer this person about her career change? What form of treatment would be most appropriate for this patient? And so on. Here again, a thorough knowledge and understanding of the quality and quantity of data available about the test and its relationship with other measures is essential if one is to provide the right kind of decision support.

Other Forms of Assessment

As has been stressed earlier in this introduction, statistically-based tests are just one in the repertoire of techniques and instruments professionals can use in decision-making. 'Informal' methods of assessment – interviews, check-lists unsupported by data, observation – are almost always used in association with test scores as a basis for decision-making.

The Assessment Library will consider non-psychometric techniques and publications in relevant volumes. Chapter 6 of this volume provides a brief introduction to other forms of assessment.

Who Can Use these Tests?

Wrong decisions can cause harm to some people who are subject to them. Wrong decisions, based on the misinterpretation of precise, numerical test data can cause even more damage, because it is less easy to refute them. Statistically-based tests, as has been noted, are 'innocuous' on the surface, hiding a statistical technology that may be quite complex. Without some degree of knowledge, it would be easy to mistake a test for a party game and vice versa. For these reasons, psychometric tests are not available freely. Most test suppliers run a registration system, and will only provide tests to the professionals who are qualified to use them – by virtue either of their initial professional training or of on-the-job courses dealing with specific tests or testing techniques.

Reading this book will not qualify you to use more tests than you already have access to. However, it may give you an insight into the contribution this kind of assessment can make to your job and help you to find out which tests you have access to and which tests you would like to have access to after appropriate training.

Conclusions

Properly used, psychometric tests can provide you with valuable additional information with which to help people. Reading a book of this kind, concerned as it is with abstract theory and technique, it is easy to forget the point of the whole exercise. Psychometrics might seem technical and abstract at times, but its purpose is a profoundly practical one: to help make better judgements about people, for their benefit and yours. In order to use any instrument well, you need to know its strengths and limitations: what it is good at doing and what it is not good at doing. You also need to develop skill in its use. Human beings are very complex, dynamic phenomena who seem at times to defy assessment. The data from psychometric tests do, however, provide a means of improving the quality and quantity of the information on which you have to base your assessments.

References

BLINKHORN, S.F. (1985). *Graduate and managerial assessment: Manual and User's Guide.* Windsor: NFER-NELSON.

KARSON, S. & O'DELL, J.W.O. (1976). *Clinical use of the 16PF. Institute for personality and ability testing.* Champaign, Illinois: IPAT.

KRUG, S. (1981). *Interpreting 16PF patterns.* Champaign, Illinois: IPAT.

Measuring Differences between People

David Bartram

In this and the following chapter, we will look at some fundamental concepts used by test constructors. If you are going to use test results as the basis for important decisions about people, it is very important to have a good grasp of these concepts. Do not worry if you do not fully understand everything in these introductory chapters first time through. A good strategy is to read these chapters first, then go on to the more applied ones and then come back to these later. Not only will you find that some grasp of the theory provides a good framework for understanding the applications, but also that knowledge of the applications and practical issues will, in turn, make the theory seem more relevant and understandable. It will be useful to have some paper, a calculator and a ruler to hand when reading these chapters. Reworking some of the examples will help your understanding.

In Chapter 3 we will discuss two issues which lie at the very heart of psychometrics: those of *validity* and *reliability* – of how we decide what we are measuring and how accurately we are measuring it. Before we can do that though, we need to learn about some of the psychometrician's basic measuring tools. These tools have been developed over the past century to provide a means of dealing with the measurement and interpretation of the variables in which we are interested. In this chapter we will focus on the measurement process itself and the techniques used to assess variation and correlation.

I have mentioned the term 'measurement' in this and the preceding chapter. Psychometrics is primarily to do with numerical systems of grading or measurement and the manipulation of these numbers. Hence the large amount of statistics in these next two chapters.

Some properties (height, length, numbers of right answers) seem easy to measure numerically. In other cases it might seem inappropriate – and dehumanizing to ascribe numbers to complex human phenomena. Yet even when we use words to make judgements (this person is *more* X than that person; this is a *very severe* case of X) we are, in effect, grading. The task of psychometrics is to turn such judgements into a form (numbers) that can be examined objectively for their accuracy, where their unconscious preconceptions can be removed so that we end up with a more accurate statement about the situation.

Such numbers might appear precise, yet be worthless in practice. So, in the process of interpretation we turn the numbers back into words which – used in association with other information – can make a connection with the real world of people and the decisions we take about them.

Variation

VARIABLES

People differ from each other in many different ways: physically, emotionally, intellectually, culturally and so on. Any particular property or characteristic on which people differ (or on which the same person differs from time to time) may be called a *variable*. Height, age, sex, anxiety, spatial ability and number of 'O' level passes are all examples of variables.

The defining characteristic of a variable is that a given person can only have one value on it at any one time. Thus, someone could weigh 150 lbs and be 5'8" tall or weigh 140 lbs and be 4'10" tall (as, in each case the person is being described in terms of two values on two different variables), but they could not be both 5'8" tall and also 4'10" tall, or weigh both 150 lbs and weigh 140 lbs. At any point in time, they must be one or the other.

Variables are typically divided into three main classes: *nominal*, *ordinal* and *scalar*.

Nominal variables are those used for naming things which cannot be ordered either discretely or continuously along some underlying scale. For example: occupation, treatment diagnosis and the names of 'A' level subject passes are all examples of nominal variables.

Ordinal variables are those with values that can be ranked. Number of 'A' level passes is an ordinal variable as it represents a scale with values that can be ranked: 'one "A" level' is more than 'none', and 'two "A" levels' is more than 'one'.

Scalar variables are measured by some form of 'independent' measurement process or instrument which can be used to assign values to people or things. If we say someone's height is 5'8" we are using a scalar variable as we have used a measurement procedure (for example, a ruler marked in equal sized intervals) which is independent of the person being measured. In effect all scalar measurement processes are based on counting. Reaction time, if we are measuring in seconds, involves counting the number of seconds elapsing between two points in time. Height, if we are measuring in centimetres, involves counting the number of centimetres from someone's feet to the top of their head. Similarly, the scores people gain on psychometric tests are typically counts of the number of items to which they have responded correctly, or the number of statements with which they have agreed and so on.

All the statistics discussed in this chapter (for instance, mean, standard deviation, correlation), which are computed from measures obtained using psychometric assessment instruments, assume that the instruments are measuring scalar variables.

MEASUREMENT PROCESSES

Most of the variables we are used to dealing with seem to be relatively 'concrete' and tangible. For example 'height': we all feel we know what we are talking about when we talk about someone's height. But if we talk about his or her intellectual ability, we might be a bit more doubtful. Equally, unless we get involved in major surgery, we have to deduce major brain damage caused by a stroke from certain outward behaviours; unless we have a crystal ball, we have to predict future job success from answers and activities that we can record now. However, in all these cases, the process of measuring involves making stipulations about how we should do the 'counting' when we take measurements.

Let us look in some detail at what is involved in measuring how tall someone is. What do we need to do? First, we need to define what it is we are trying to find out. For the moment, we can say that a person's height is the distance – in a straight line – from the ground to the top of their head when they are standing upright without shoes on. What we will need is a measuring instrument – scaled to measure linear extent – that will allow us to quantify this distance. Fortunately there are standards that define units of distance: the Imperial standard for feet and inches, or the SI (Système International d'Unités) metric scales. We will need a suitable 'ruler' – for example, a straight line marked off in centimetres – that we can place upright beside the person. We can then count the number of centimetre units from the floor to the top of their head. In practice, of course, 'rulers' do the counting for you, having the counts marked on each division of the scale. Having done all this, we now have a measure of height (let us say it is 175 cm).

Reconsider what is required for what seems like a very simple operation:

1. Define a set of conditions under which the measurement is to be made.
2. Define a measuring procedure.
3. Choose an appropriate measurement scale.
4. Carry out the measuring operation.

For measuring physical characteristics – like height – none of this is terribly difficult. But it is important to think very clearly about what is going on in simple situations if we are to understand what is involved in measuring more complex characteristics.

Take, for example, the precision of our measurement. We could say a person is under two metres tall, or that they are 175 cm tall or we might want to say they are 1753.678 mm tall. The first of these is rather uninformative – as most people are under two metres tall. The last may look very 'accurate', but if you have ever tried to measure someone's height, you will appreciate that its accuracy is spurious. Simple variations in the way a person stands and holds his or her head will make it very unlikely that you would get exactly 1753 mm (let alone be able to actually read a scale marked in thousandths of a millimetre!) every time you measured them. (Furthermore, people 'shrink' slightly between the time they get up and go to bed due to gravity compression effects.) So, instead of getting one particular height value, what is more likely is that you would get a range of values between 174 and 176 cm.

Whatever actual value we obtain, we know that it is not possible to say with absolute confidence, that it *is* the person's height – because the next time we measure it, we are likely to get a slightly different value. Yet we feel it is quite reasonable to assume that they 'have' a height that is relatively stable – that will not vary randomly from moment to moment – and that it is useful to obtain measurements of it – even if those measurements are imprecise.

This assumption forms the premise that underlies what is known as Classical Test Theory. Quite simply, it is argued that, people possess specific amounts of underlying or latent 'traits' (ability, height or whatever). If we could directly measure this specific amount, we would have their *true score*. In practice, for the reasons we have discussed above, we can only ever measure these traits indirectly and imprecisely. The scores which we obtain are termed *fallible* scores and are regarded as consisting of the true score plus or minus some amount of error. This divide between what we actually can measure, given limitations of time, practicality and human perception – and what, in an ideal world we could measure – is central to psychometrics. Assuming these errors are random (so that sometimes the height we record is too much and sometimes too little), if we take enough measurements and then find their average, the errors should tend to cancel out.

Suppose we obtained ten measurements of the same person's height (see Box 2.1). Our best estimate of the person's 'true' height is the familiar mean or arithmetic average of these values. That is, the sum of all the values (17,520) divided by the number of values (10). As well as the ten measurements, Box 2.1 shows the deviations of those measures about their mean or average (that is, the differences between each value and the mean). If these deviations are added together, their sum will be zero. In fact, this is a defining property of the familiar average or mean. This implies that if we take the mean to represent the person's 'true' height, then the average measurement error we make will be zero (the sum of the deviations divided by the number of measurements) as the positive and negative errors will cancel each other out.

MEASURES OF VARIATION: THE STANDARD DEVIATION AND VARIANCE

While the mean or average of a set of numbers is a fairly familiar statistic, we need some way of describing the degree to which each number in our sample varies around the mean. The measure we use is called the *Standard Deviation* (SD). As one would expect, the standard deviation is derived from the deviations of the measurements about their mean. As we saw though, we cannot simply average these deviations (as they always add up to zero). What we do to get round this problem is: square all the deviations (so they all become positive); add up the squared deviations and divide the total by the number of values; finally take the square root of this to get back to the same units we started with.

In the process of computing the standard deviation, we actually produce two other important statistics: the sum of squares and the variance. If you look at the data in Box 2.1, you will see that the sum of the squared devia-tions is 124. This value is called the sum of squares (which is short for 'sum of the squared deviations about the mean'). Just as the sample mean or average is derived by dividing the sum of the values (17,520) by the num-ber of values (10), so the sample variance is obtained by dividing the sum of squares (124) by the number of values (10). When we do this, we get a value of 12.4 for the above data. (As the variance is the average of the sum of squares, it is sometimes referred to as the mean square – which is short for 'mean of the squared deviations about the mean'.) From the variance (12.4) we can then obtain the SD by taking the square root (3.52).

It is important to note that the standard deviation is measured in exactly the same units as our original data, and represents a distance along the measuring scale (3.25 mm height in the case of the data in Box 2.1). The sample variance, on the other hand, represents the area of a square (12.4 sq mm for the data in Box 2.1) whose sides are each one SD long. Thus, the variance and the SD are really two ways of describing the same thing. We will see later that both these statistics are very important.

MEASURING SAMPLES AND ESTIMATING POPULATIONS

In Box 2.1 we see an example in which a sample of measurements was taken of a person's height. In fact we could go on measuring that person's height forever, hoping to get a more and more accurate estimate of their *true height*. The set of all the possible measures we could take (whether of height or reaction time or ability to read) is known as the *population of measures*. Since it is not advisable (or possible) in practice, to try to take the entire population of measures, psychometric tests, like most other measurement instruments, take a sample of measures and from that sample make estimates about the properties of the population from which the sample was drawn.

Thus, a lot of the statistical techniques described in this book are de-signed to provide you and the test constructor with a sort of 'short cut'. For example, rather than trying to measure everybody, the test constructor measures a sample of people who are representative of everybody and provides you – in the test manual – with the information you need to know how well that sample represents the population. This means that when you measure somebody you can compare their scores against everyone else in the population – even though most of the population will actually never have been measured.

It should be noted that in psychometrics 'population' does not mean 'all the inhabitants of a country'. It has a very special meaning and refers to that set of things (people, test questions, and so on) that might have been chosen when we selected a sample.

In Box 2.1 we computed the variance and standard deviation (SD) of a *sample* of ten measurements of someone's height. If we wish to measure the standard deviation and variance of the whole population from which a sample is drawn we must use a different method. There is a reason for this.

The variance and standard deviation of a sample tend to underestimate the variance and standard deviation of a whole population – in other words, we are underestimating the extremes of height measures we could

Box 2.1
Estimating population variance and Standard Deviation: method

Raw Scores for the person's height (mm)	Deviations from the mean or average (mm)	Squared deviations from the mean (square mm)
1756	+4	16
1748	−4	16
1751	−1	1
1752	0	0
1749	−3	9
1746	−6	36
1758	+6	36
1753	+1	1
1755	+3	9
1752	0	0
Sum or Total 17,520	0	Sum of squares 124
Mean or 1752	0	Mean square or sample variance 12.4

10 measurements are taken of a person's height in millimetres. These are totalled and the average is found.

The average is then taken away from each individual measurement (e.g. 1756–1752) to find the deviations of each measurement about the mean. These are totalled and the mean or average is found. These last two statistics – as can be seen above – will also be 0.

To find the 'standard deviation' which describes the way the sample measurements we have taken vary about the mean as a whole we go through a number of steps.

1. Multiply each deviation by itself (i.e. $+4 \times +4 = 16, -1 \times -1 = 1$) to get squared deviations in square mm.

2. Total these figures.

3. Find the average by dividing the total by the number of measurements (i.e. $124 \div 10) = 12.4$. This figure is known as the 'mean square' or sample variance.

4. Since all the above figures are in square mm, we find the square root of the sample variance to find the standard deviation.
$$\sqrt{12.4} = 3.52 \text{ mm}$$
The standard deviation of this sample of measurements is 3.52 mm.

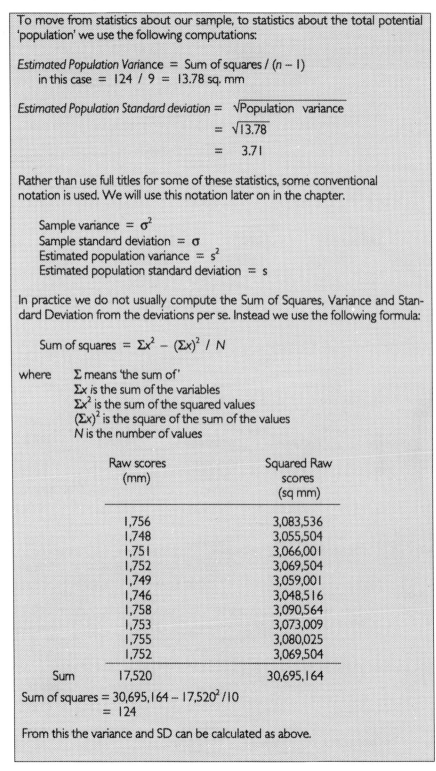

To move from statistics about our sample, to statistics about the total potential 'population' we use the following computations:

Estimated Population Variance = Sum of squares / $(n - 1)$
    in this case = $124 / 9 = 13.78$ sq. mm

Estimated Population Standard deviation = $\sqrt{\text{Population variance}}$
$$= \sqrt{13.78}$$
$$= 3.71$$

Rather than use full titles for some of these statistics, some conventional notation is used. We will use this notation later on in the chapter.

Sample variance = σ^2
Sample standard deviation = σ
Estimated population variance = s^2
Estimated population standard deviation = s

In practice we do not usually compute the Sum of Squares, Variance and Standard Deviation from the deviations per se. Instead we use the following formula:

Sum of squares = $\Sigma x^2 - (\Sigma x)^2 / N$

where Σ means 'the sum of'
    Σx is the sum of the variables
    Σx^2 is the sum of the squared values
    $(\Sigma x)^2$ is the square of the sum of the values
    N is the number of values

Raw scores (mm)	Squared Raw scores (sq mm)
1,756	3,083,536
1,748	3,055,504
1,751	3,066,001
1,752	3,069,504
1,749	3,059,001
1,746	3,048,516
1,758	3,090,564
1,753	3,073,009
1,755	3,080,025
1,752	3,069,504
Sum 17,520	30,695,164

Sum of squares = $30,695,164 - 17,520^2 / 10$
$$= 124$$

From this the variance and SD can be calculated as above.

arrive at if we kept on measuring the person forever. An extreme case will help to show why.

If we take one measure (say 1756 mm in Box 2.1) and set about our calculations we will find that the sum of the scores is 1756 and their mean or average is 1756. The deviation from the mean is 0, the squared deviation about the mean is 0 and the sum of squares, sample variance and standard deviation will all be a resounding zero. Given that the population of measures does vary, then this will be a gross underestimate of the sample variation.

As we take more measures (increase our sample size) so the amount of underestimation decreases. At the other extremes, if we had the full population of measures available (that is, the sample *was* the population), then the sample variance would no longer underestimate the population variance.

In practice we can remove the 'bias' from the sample variance if we want to estimate the population variance. Instead of dividing the sum of squares by the number of values in the sample (n), we divide it by one less than the number of values ($n-1$). If you look at Box 2.1, you will see that the sample variance is 12.4 (that is 124/10), while the estimated population variances is slightly larger (that is, $124/(10-1)=13.78$). The value, $n-1$, is technically known as the degrees of freedom of the sum of squares.

THE NORMAL DISTRIBUTION

The more measures we take of some characteristic from the same person, the better our estimate of that person's 'true' score. Similarly, the more people we measure from a population, the better we are able to estimate the mean and SD for scores in that population. In theory we could go on increasing the number of measures we take until we had an infinitely large number (as we are talking 'in theory' we can leave aside the practical problem that both we and the person we are measuring would have died an infinitely long time ago!).

Figure 2.1 shows a frequency distribution, presented in the form of a histogram, of the scores of 216 people on a scale from a mood assessment inventory. The number of people obtaining each of the possible scores is shown by the height of each column. It is typical of the sort of distribution one would obtain for a wide variety of other measures. While the outline of this histogram is not very smooth, as we add measures from more and more people, the shape of the distribution gradually tends towards a smooth 'bell-shape'. This shape of distribution – or one very like it – is found for a wide variety of both physical and psychological traits. It is fairly obvious to see why. In the case of height you very rarely see people who are 6'10" or 3'6": most cases fall within a range of 5' to 6'; similarly, you meet very few totally extravert people and very few totally introvert. Most people are a mix of the two. Because of this it is termed the 'normal frequency distribution' or just the 'normal curve' – see Figure 2.2. As we could never take the infinite number of measurements needed to build it up, it is a theoretical distribution. However, with relatively few measures, frequency distributions can look very similar to this. (The various measurement systems shown in Figure 2.2 underneath the distribution will be explained shortly. Ignore them for the moment.)

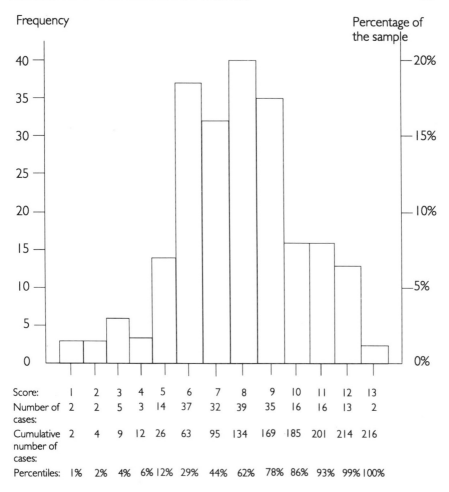

Score:	1	2	3	4	5	6	7	8	9	10	11	12	13
Number of cases:	2	2	5	3	14	37	32	39	35	16	16	13	2
Cumulative number of cases:	2	4	9	12	26	63	95	134	169	185	201	214	216
Percentiles:	1%	2%	4%	6%	12%	29%	44%	62%	78%	86%	93%	99%	100%

Figure 2.1: Frequency distribution of scores on a mood assessment inventory

The histogram depicts a frequency distribution (number of cases for each score) of scores for 216 people on a mood assessment inventory. The height of each bar represents the number of people (the frequency) obtaining each score. The right-hand vertical axis represents the frequencies as percentages of the total number of people (216). This also reflects the probability of someone obtaining a particular score. For example, as 18 per cent of people obtain a score of 8, the probability of someone obtaining a score of 8 is 0.18.

Beneath the horizontal axis is the cumulated number of cases, and the cumulative percentage of cases (percentiles) for each score: for example, 95 people (44 per cent of the sample) obtain a score of 7 or less; 201 (93 per cent) obtain a score of 11 or less and so on.

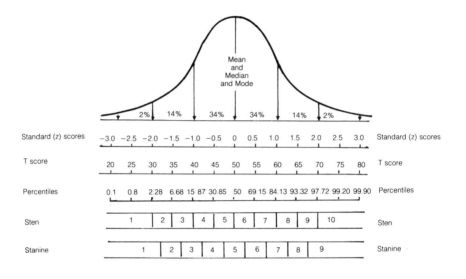

Figure 2.2: Normal distribution curve

The normal distribution curve has been divided into sections each one standard deviation wide. The approximate percentage of cases falling in each section is shown (that is, 2 per cent between z-score = minus infinity and z-score = −2; 14 per cent between z-score = −2 and z-score = −1 and so on). Thus 84 per cent (or 84.13 per cent, to be exact) of the distribution lies below z-score = +1 (that is, 2% + 14% + 34% + 34%).

Beneath the z-score scale is shown the T-score scale and the percentile values of each 0.5 SD intervals shown on the two scales. Thus, a z-score of 1.5 is equivalent to a T-score of 65 and, for a normal distribution, both scores are at the 93rd percentile. Whereas the T-scale uses 0.1 SD size intervals, the Sten ('Standard-Ten') and Stanine ('Standard-Nine') scales use 0.5 SD size intervals. Both the latter scales have an SD of 2.0 (that is, two intervals per z-score). For Stens, the mean of the scale is 5.5, while for Stanines it is 5.0.

Unlike z-scores (which can range, in theory, from minus to plus infinity), T-scores, Stens and Stanines have minimum (one) and maximum values (100 for T-scores, 10 for Stens and 9 for Stanines).

Not all characteristics have 'normal' distributions. Frequently, though, these different shapes can be described as distortions of normal curves; sometimes they are 'skewed' one way or the other; sometimes the top of the distribution may be flattened or very pointed. Nevertheless, it is often useful to assume that the amounts of the property we wish to measure which people possess (that is, their 'true' scores) have a normal distribution across the population even if the measures we take (that is, their fallible scores) have a distribution that has been distorted in some way – either by the sampling of items or by the measurement process. For these and other reasons, many psychometric procedures are based on the assumption that the measures they are dealing with are drawn from an underlying normal distribution.

Why bother making this assumption? The answer is that the normal distribution provides a *standard reference distribution* with known properties. As it is symmetrical, its mean, median and mode are all the same. Thus, not only is its mean or average the point about which the variance is minimized (as we showed in our discussion of Box 2.1), it is also the point that divides the bottom 50 per cent of measures from the top 50 per cent (the median) and it is the value with the highest probability occurring (the mode). The important point about this, as we will see later, is that it allows us to compare measures of very different attributes – spatial ability and verbal reasoning, for instance.

PROBABILITIES, PERCENTILES AND NORMAL DISTRIBUTIONS

For an actual frequency distribution (constructed from the actual measures we have taken of a real sample), the height at any point is simply the number of measures (that is, the frequency) obtained. The theoretical normal distribution, however, is a *probability distribution*. A probability distribution can easily be constructed from a frequency distribution by dividing each frequency on the vertical scale by the total number of cases in the sample and expressing this as a percentage. In Figure 2.1 the scale on the right of the histogram gives the percentage (for example, around 6 per cent obtain a score of 5) of the sample obtaining each scale score. If we turn these percentages into proportions (for example, 6 per cent becomes 0.06), and then add all the proportions together, the total will be one (just as the total of the percentages would be 100 per cent).

A probability distribution is simply one in which the heights of each column are expressed as proportions rather than frequencies. The proportion of people who obtain a particular score represents our best estimate of the probability of that score (that is, the likelihood of that score occurring). Thus, if 6 per cent of people obtain a score of 5, we can say that the likelihood of someone getting a score of 5 is 0.06.

Suppose we want to find the likelihood of someone obtaining a score *at least as big as* 8. From the information in Figure 2.1, we know that 134, or 62 per cent of the people, get a score between 1 and 8. Hence the likelihood of someone obtaining a score of between 1 and 8 is 0.62. Beneath the measurement scale on Figure 2.1 is another scale, showing the percentages of people who obtain scores at least as big as each of the values. This is called a percentile scale. For any scale, given enough data, we can translate 'raw scores' into percentile scores in this manner. Indeed, given enough data and a fine enough measuring scale, we can draw up a table that allows us to 'translate' any raw scores into a percentile. Many test manuals contain such tables (for example, the Graduate and Managerial Assessment test manual). Others use scales based on percentiles. For example the AH series of ability tests use a 5-point grading scheme where:

1. The top 10 per cent of scores are classed as grade A,
2. The next 20 per cent as grade B,
3. The next 40 per cent as grade C,
4. The next 20 per cent as grade D,
5. And the lowest 10 per cent as grade E.

Percentile scores have a number of advantages. First, they have an immediate meaning in terms of a person's score in relation to those of everyone else. Second, if we plot a distribution of percentile scores, it would be symmetrical with a mean of 50 (since the scores range between 0 and 100), regardless of the shape of the original frequency distribution. However, it would not be a normal distribution as it would be too stretched at each end. In terms of raw scores the difference between, say, the 10th and 20th, or the 80th and 90th percentiles is much larger than the difference between the 40th and 50th or 50th and 60th. However, we can easily transform a percentile scale into one which is normally distributed.

Above we saw how, for a probability distribution, the sum of the heights of all the columns was one. Another way of putting this is to say that if we drew a continuous line around the outline shape of the histogram, the total area inside the line would be equal to one. As the normal distribution is just a special type of probability distribution, so the total area underneath a normal curve is also always one.

As well as having a 'standard' area of one, the normal distribution's mean and variance are also standardized: the mean is zero and the variance is one. Thus, the normal distribution is a symmetrical smooth curve containing an area equal to one, with a mean of zero and a variance (and hence also an SD) of one. The points one SD above and below the mean (known as the points of inflexion) are actually where the curve changes from being concave to being convex.

We can refer to any particular point along a normally distributed scale as being so many standard deviations (SDs) above (for example, +1.46) or below (for example, −2.15) the mean. Tables have been produced that give the areas under different parts of a normal curve. From these we can find the probability of obtaining scores that are either less than or greater than any particular value along the measurement scale. In Figure 2.2 some of these values are shown – for example, you can see that 84 per cent (2 per cent + 14 per cent + 34 per cent and 34 per cent) of scores will be less than one SD above the mean. A more complete list of values is given in the Appendix.

Z-SCORES

Scores measured in standard deviation units are called *z-scores*. For example a z-score of +1.3 is 1.3 SDs above the mean; while one of −2.56 is 2.56 SDs below the mean.

We can convert measures on any scale into z-scores if we first subtract the mean from each value (to obtain the deviations about the mean) and then divide the deviations from the mean by the SD.

Z-score = (Raw score − Mean)/SD

In Box 2.2 we have taken the basic data in Box 2.1 and added z-scores. Here a height of 1760 mm would be equivalent to a z-score of +2.27. If we look that up in normal distribution tables (Appendix) we find the chances of getting a value as large as this would be very small – less than 0.02, or 2 per cent, if the data are normally distributed.

When we compute z-scores for the sample of ten height measures shown in Box 2.2 we can see that the mean of the z-scores is zero; the sum of squares for the z-scores equals the sample size (10); and the variance and SD are both equal to 1. We can just as easily convert back from z-scores to 'raw scores'. If the SD is 3.52 and the mean is 1752 then a z-score of +2.35 is the same as a raw score of:

Raw score = Mean + (SD × z-score)
          = 1752 + (3.52 × 2.35)
          = 1760.27 mm

When we convert raw scores to z-scores and back again we do not change the shape of the distribution – we simply change the mean and SD of the measurement scale. So if our raw score distribution is skewed to the left, converting the z-scores simply changes the mean to zero and the SD to one: the distribution of z-scores will be just as skewed as the raw scores.

The statement that 34 per cent of the distribution lies between the mean and +1 SD, and 34 per cent between the mean and −1 SD, is *only* true for a normal distribution (such as Figure 2.2), a skewed distribution will have a larger percentage one side of the mean than the other.

NORMALIZED STANDARD SCORES

It was pointed out earlier that, even if the measures we obtain of some characteristic have a skewed distribution, it is often convenient to assume that these measures derive from some underlying trait that has a *normal distribution*. It is also desirable to transform non-normal distributions into normal ones as we then know that mean, median and mode all have the same value, and that dispersion about this central point is symmetrical. This makes comparison between measures easier, which is important when you are looking to assess a person over a range of abilities and look at patterns of scores.

When the raw score distribution is clearly not normal, it can be transformed – or 'normalized'. The procedure is very simple, making use of what we know about how to produce percentile scores from any distribution and the relationship between percentiles and normally distributed z-scores.

Suppose we have obtained scores on a new test from a standardization sample of 400 people. We can take all the scores and rank order from lowest to highest. Every four scores up the rank order would represent another 1 per cent of the sample. So, the score falling between the first 40

Box 2.2

Estimating population variance and Standard Deviation: example

| | Deviations from the mean | | Squared deviations from the mean | |
Raw scores (mm)	Raw scores (mm)	z-scores	Raw scores (sq. mm)	z-scores
1756	+4	+1.1359	16	1.29032
1748	−4	−1.1359	16	1.29032
1751	−1	−0.2840	1	0.08064
1752	0	0.00	0	0.000
1749	−3	−0.8519	9	0.72581
1746	−6	−1.7039	36	2.90323
1758	+6	+1.7039	36	2.90323
1753	+1	+0.2840	1	0.08064
1755	+3	+0.8519	9	0.72581
1752	0	0.00	0	0.000

| Sum 17520 | 0 | 0.00 | Sum of squares 124 | 10.00000 |
| Mean 1752 | 0 | 0.00 | Mean square or 12.4 sample variance | 1.00000 |

Sum of squares = 124 sq mm (for z-scores = 10)
Sample variance: $\sigma^2 = 12.40$ sq. mm (for z-scores = 1)
Sample SD: $\sigma = 3.52$ mm (for z-scores = 1)
Estimated population variance: $s^2 = 13.78$ sq. mm
Estimated population SD: $S = 3.71$ mm

and the 41st in the rank order would be the tenth 'percentile', that between scores 100 and 101 would be the 25th percentile and so on. In this way, each raw score can be 'translated' into a percentile score.

As already mentioned, many psychometric tests use these percentile scores directly. However, once raw scores have been turned into percentiles, the percentiles can be turned into z-scores (using the normal distribution tables – see Appendix).

If we obtain z-scores by first turning raw scores into percentiles and then finding the z-scores for each percentile score, then the z-scores will be normally distributed even if the raw scores were not. This is necessarily the case as each percentile score is converted into a z-score by using normal distribution tables. It is important to note, however, that when z-scores are obtained *directly* from raw scores (by subtracting the mean and then dividing by the SD) these z-scores will have exactly the same distribution as the raw scores had.

Scores based on z-scores which have been obtained *indirectly* – through the intermediate step of conversion to percentiles – are called 'normalized scores'.

By using *normalized standardized scores* we can make direct comparisons between measurements of all sorts of different things – for example verbal reasoning and spatial reasoning – each of which may have different raw score means and SDs and different distributions. Saying someone scores 97 on Verbal Reasoning and 18 on Spatial Reasoning is relatively uninformative. Saying they obtained z-scores of +1.2 and +1.3 on the two tests tells us a great deal more: first that they perform at about the same level on both tests and second, that they are in the top 10 per cent of the population on which the tests were standardized.

Apart from z-scores (with their mean of zero and SD of one), there are a range of other 'standard' scores. Some of the more common ones are shown on Figure 2.2. In each case scores on these scales are easily derived from z-scores. The z-score is multiplied by the relevant SD, the relevant mean is added to the product, and the resulting value is rounded to the nearest whole number. For example: a z-score of −1.96 is equivalent to a T-score of 30, and a Sten of 2 and a Stanine of 1. (Take a bit of time studying the notes in Figure 2.2 and work through some of these scores.)

In general T-scores, Stens and Stanines are obtained from normalized distributions (using percentile transformations) and hence are referred to as 'normalized standard scores'. However, they may also be calculated directly from raw score means and SDs, in which case they will only be normally distributed if the raw scores are.

THE STANDARD DEVIATION AND THE STANDARD ERROR

So far we have talked about the mean and SD of a distribution. We have also noted that any sample of actual measures that we take can be considered as having been drawn from a much larger population of possible measures. What does the mean and SD of our sample tell us about the mean and SD of the population it came from? This is a very important question: psychometrics is very much concerned with the problem of estimating unknown values from samples of known ones.

Suppose that for a large population the mean score on an IQ test battery is 100 with an SD of 15. If we took a sample of 50 people from this population and measured their IQs, we would not expect to get an average of exactly 100 or an SD of exactly 15, but we would regard those as being the most likely values. If we took other samples of 50 people, before measuring each of them, our 'best guess' about the mean IQs of each sample would be 100 with an SD of 15. We would not expect to be exactly right in our guesses, and sometimes we should find the mean was a bit less, sometimes a bit more than we expected.

Suppose we continued taking samples of 50 people and calculating the mean or average IQ of each sample until we had two or three hundred sample means. As well as producing a frequency distribution of the actual measures we could also produce one of all the means. The mean of these sample means should be a very good estimate of the population mean. The standard deviation of the sample means would indicate the extent to which sample means tended to vary from the population mean. This SD is called the Standard Error of the Mean (SE_{mean}) as it indicates the size of the error we would tend to make if we use a sample mean as an estimate of the population mean. There is a very simple relationship between the estimated population variance (S^2), the size of a sample drawn from the population (N) and the Standard Error of the mean of that sample (SE_{mean}).

$$SE_{mean} = \sqrt{(S^2/N)}$$

Since the standard deviation is the square root of the population variance (see Box 2.1), this can be expressed as

$$SE_{mean} = SD/\sqrt{N}$$

For the IQ example:

$$SE_{mean} = 15/\sqrt{50}$$
$$= 2.12$$

What this says is that if we look at the distribution of the means of a very large number of samples (each containing 50 people), the SD of that distribution should be 2.12. We know (from normal distribution tables) that the probability of a measure falling within plus or minus one SD of the mean is 0.68 (68 per cent). Thus, if we take a sample of 50 people, we can be 68 per cent confident that its mean will lie between 97.88 and 102.12 (that is, plus or minus one standard error). Another way of looking at this is to say that if we took 100 samples, each of 50 people, 0.95 (95 per cent) of the sample means should lie within plus or minus 1.96 SEs of the mean (that is, between 95.84 and 104.16).

Calculate the SE of the mean for sample sizes of 10 and 500 for the IQ example. Notice how, as the sample size increases, so the sample mean becomes a much more accurate estimate of the population mean.

I hope you will now begin to see how psychometric techniques provide you with both a rigorous way of treating scores and an element of quantifiable doubt about their accuracy. While the SE_{mean} might be more immediately relevant to the test *constructor* than the test *user*, such statements of confidence about a test's accuracy are crucial when viewing an individual's score on the test.

In practice we do not know the population mean and SD and so have to use this argument in reverse. We take a sample of 50 people and find that their mean IQ is 98 and the SD is 14. As this is the only information we have, 98 is our best estimate of what the population mean is and 14 is our best estimate of the population SD. Similarly $14/\sqrt{(50)} = 1.98$ is our best estimate of the SE of the mean as an estimate of the population mean. We would conclude that we can be about 95 per cent confident that the population mean lies in the interval 94 to 102.

Co-variation: Correlation and Regression

So far we have talked about 'univariate' distributions – that is, distributions of measures on a single variable. We have seen how the location and spread of such a distribution can be 'specified' by its mean and standard deviation (SDs) and how the raw scores can be transformed into a z-score distribution which will always have a mean of zero and a variance of one.

We have also seen how, for many variables, the shape of the distribution of measures tends to approximate the normal curve.

For those that do not, it is generally possible to 'normalize' the raw score distribution by turning the raw scores into percentiles and then the percentiles into z-scores. The value of working with z-scores rather than raw scores will become more apparent as we move from a consideration of univariate distributions (distributions of scores on one variable) to bivariate and multivariate ones (distributions concerning two or more variables).

For now we will focus on bivariate distributions. For single distributions, we could describe their main characteristics in terms of the mean and SD. For two distributions we will need two means and two SDs and some measure of the relationship or co-variation between the variables.

Take a simple example. Between the ages of 1 and 16 years, age and height are positively related variables (as people get older they also get taller). It is not a perfect relationship, as not everyone grows at the same rate, but in general given someone's age we are quite good at guessing what their height is likely to be. Conversely, given their height, we are likely to be pretty accurate at guessing their age. We can do this because we have a lot of experience observing the relationship between these two variables.

In psychometrics, we cannot rely on our experience to estimate values of one variable from observations of another. This is so for a number of reasons. First, because such experience and what we learn from it is idiosyncratic (some people are likely to be better at estimating height from age than others). Second, such guesses are not 'quantitative': we are not able to specify their degree of accuracy. Finally, psychometrics is designed to help us with traits that cannot be directly observed or measured in the way height and age can.

Psychometricians have developed a number of different methods of 'quantifying' the degree of relationship (or degree of co-variation) between variables. The most widely used measures of co-variation all derive from a common computational method: the Pearson product-moment correlation coefficient. To avoid saying 'Pearson product-moment correlation coefficient' too often, it is customary simply to refer to a *correlation coefficient* and talk about 'the correlation' between two variables. Whenever we do so, though, it is important to remember that we are talking about one particular way of measuring the relationship between variables.

An understanding of correlation (and the related notion of regression) is important as so many crucial aspects of test construction depend on it – including reliability and certain types of validity that are dealt with in the next chapter. What is important, however, is not the ability to calculate correlation coefficients – you may never need to do that – but an understanding of what they are and what they can tell you about two variables.

LINEAR AND NON-LINEAR RELATIONSHIPS

Correlation is used to measure the degree to which changes in one variable are associated with changes in another. Like age and height, it may be that as one increases so the other increases (this is a positive relationship), or the two may vary in opposite directions (a negative relationship such as perhaps acquisition of expensive clothes and amount of money left in your current account). The sign of a relationship (whether it is '+' or '−') tells us whether the variables co-vary in the same or opposing directions. The size of the relationship tells us how closely associated they are. Correlation coefficients can vary from a (theoretical) maximum value of either $+1$ or -1 to a minimum value of 0 (where there is no correlation).

The techniques we will be discussing in this chapter relate to a special type of relationship between variables: a straight-line or rectilinear one. A rectilinear relationship is one where the relationship is the same for all points along the scales. The graphs shown in Figures 2.3a to 2.3d all show 'perfect relationships' between two variables (X and Y). These are perfect because for each value of X there are a discrete number of exact values of Y (and vice versa). The lines drawn on the figures represent all the possible pairs of X and Y values.

While all these figures depict perfect relationships between the two variables, only one is a straight-line or rectilinear function (2.3a). Figure 2.3b shows a curvilinear relationship in which as X increases Y always increases, but the rate of increase changes (it 'accelerates' as X gets bigger). Figures 2.3a and b both show positive relationships between X and Y.

Figure 2.3c is different in that for part of the function there is a negative relationship between X and Y while for the remainder the relationship is positive.

Figure 2.3d shows an even more complex function. Fortunately, the relationships we come across between psychological and physical variables are rarely more complex than the U-shape one. Furthermore, in practice a very large part of variance that variables share can be accounted for by simple rectilinear relationships. Techniques do, however, exist for quantifying the non-linear relationships between variables. These are simply extensions of the methods used for linear relationships.

To repeat a point made earlier, correlation coefficients can vary from a (theoretical) maximum value of either $+1$ or -1 to a minimum value of 0. The form of correlation we will be discussing in this chapter is 'sensitive' only to rectilinear relationships. Thus a correlation of zero will be obtained when there is no rectilinear relationship between two variables even if there is some non-linear relationship. Correlations of plus or minus one are obtained when there is a perfect straight-line relationship between them. In reality, most correlations fall somewhere in between these two extremes (we shall see why in Chapter 3).

The remainder of this chapter will concentrate on explaining what correlation is, what the correlation coefficient means and how it is computed. You can, if you wish, skip over the 'computational' parts – as a test user you may never need to work out a correlation for yourself. However, it will help you to understand the information presented in test manuals if you have an idea of how the various measures are derived.

PREDICTIONS AND ERRORS OF PREDICTION

From our examination of univariate distributions we know the following:

1. The mean or average of a distribution defines the 'centre' of the distribution and is the best predictor of the value of any unknown measure taken from that distribution (as the average error of prediction will be zero if we always use the mean).

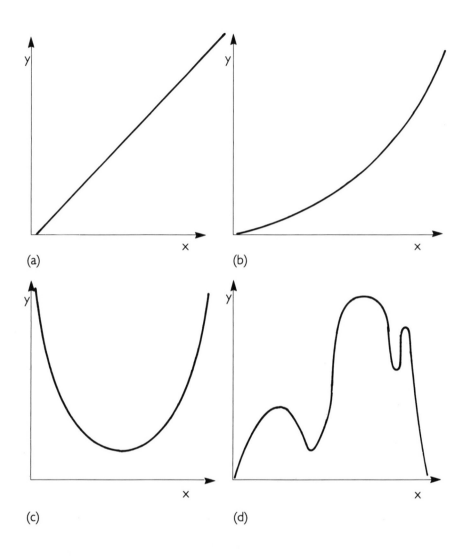

Figure 2.3: Exact relationships between x and y

Each figure shows an exact relationship between x and y. For any point along the x axis one can draw a line vertically upwards to find the value of y. In all cases, there will only be one y value for each x value. One can also draw lines horizontally from any point along the y axis to find the x value. For (a) and (b) there will only be one x value for each y. For (c) there will be two x values from some value of y, while for (d) there will be up to four different x values associated with some values of y.

2. The standard deviation indicates the spread or dispersion of values in the distribution. As it is derived from the deviations of each measure from the mean it also indicates the size of errors we would tend to make if we used the mean to predict unknown values from the distribution.
3. The SE_{mean} indicates the degree to which the means of different samples of measures from the same population will tend to vary. Specifically, it measures the size of error we tend to make in using any particular sample mean as an estimate of the population mean.

Unless there is no variance (in which case we do not have a variable) we will always make some error if we try to predict unknown values of a variable. However, by definition, using the mean of a distribution as the predicted value produces an average prediction error of zero (as the plus and minus errors will balance each other out – see Box 2.1) and also produces the smallest 'least squares' error or minimum error variance (which equals one, if we are using z-scores – see Box 2.2).

Look at the information given in Box 2.3. If you were asked to guess each of the 216 Scale 1 scores purely on the basis of the information given above, your best bet would be to estimate that each person scored 7.84 (the mean). Your predictions would then have a mean equal to the mean of the Scale (that is, 7.84) and a variance of zero (as all 216 predictions were the same). Your errors of prediction will be exactly the same as the deviations of each actual score about the mean. Hence, your errors of prediction will have a mean of zero (as the plus and minus errors will balance out) and variance of 5.32 (that is, the total sample variance). Notice how all the Scale 1 variance (5.32) would be reflected in your errors of prediction and none of it in your actual predictions (as all 216 of them were the same value: 7.84).

Clearly, one would like to do rather better with one's predictions than simply say everyone will score the same! In effect what one needs to do is increase the variance of the predictions while reducing the variance of the errors of prediction as much as possible. For the moment, it is important to appreciate that when the mean is used as the best predictor:

1. The average of the errors of prediction will be zero.
2. The variance of the errors of prediction will be equal to the variance of the measure being predicted.
3. If using z-scores rather than raw scores then the variance of the errors of prediction will be equal to one.

BIVARIATE FREQUENCY DISTRIBUTIONS

A bivariate frequency distribution is one that shows the relationship between two variables (hence 'bivariate'). How can we represent this sort of relationship? For single variables we have seen that we can create a 'flat' or two-dimensional histogram, with the horizontal axis being the measurement scale and the vertical axis being the frequency. We have also seen how a normal distribution can be represented in a similar two-dimensional

Box 2.3

Descriptive statistics for a sample of 216 people's scores on two scales of a personality inventory

	Scale 1	Scale 2
Mean	7.84	7.49
Variance	5.32	5.41
SD	2.31	2.33
N	216	216
SE$_{mean}$	0.16	0.16

If you are not sure of some of these statistics, go back to Boxes 2.1 and 2.2 and check over them again. The SE$_{mean}$ is explained on pages 25–6.

manner. For two variables we are going to have to use another dimension to represent the second variable.

Figure 2.4 shows a three-dimensional histogram and a table showing its bivariate frequency distribution (it is the data from which Box 2.3 was generated). Each possible combination of scores on Scales 1 and 2 is represented by a 'cell' in the frequency table. The number in the cell is the number of people who obtained that particular combination of scores (for example, the score of one cell has been highlighted showing that just one person scored 8 on Scale 1 and 12 on Scale 2). The cells of the table correspond to the grid on which the histogram is built. Sitting on each cell is a block whose height represents the number of people in that cell. Along the edges of both the histogram and the table are the univariate distributions for each of the scales. Look, for example, at the row of cells which relate to a score of 10 on Scale 1: the 16 people who obtained that score are made up from 2 people who got 4 on Scale 2, one who got 5, 2 who scored 7, and so on.

Notice how some cells are empty while others contain quite large numbers. From the pattern of this distribution we can see that there is a tendency for high scores on one variable to go with high scores on the other and low scores on one to go with low scores on the other. Notice how the top left and bottom right-hand corners of the table are quite empty, while the top right and bottom left contain entries. Suppose we are told that John Smith had a score of 10 on Scale 1. Given this piece of information, from the bivariate frequency distribution we can predict that his score on Scale 2 is more likely to be above than below the mean. As there is a clear positive relationship between the two scales, people who score above the mean on one scale will, on average, tend to score above the mean on the other.

SCALE 2

SCALE 1	1	2	3	4	5	6	7	8	9	10	11	12	13	Tot	%
13								1		1				2	.9
12									2	1	4	5	1	13	6.0
11						1	1	3	1	5	5			16	7.4
10				2	1		2	2	4	3	2			16	7.4
9				1		5	5	7	8	2	5	2		35	16.2
8				1	3	11	10	6	6		1	1		39	18.1
7				2	3	8	8	7	3	1				32	14.8
6				2	6	10	9	6	3	1				37	17.1
5			1	1	2	1	5	3	1					14	6.5
4		1			1			1						3	1.4
3	2	1				1		1						5	2.3
2		1	1											2	.9
1	2													2	.9
Tot	4	3	2	9	16	37	40	37	28	14	17	8	1	216	
%	1.9	1.4	.9	4.2	7.4	17.1	18.5	17.1	13.0	6.5	7.9	3.7	.5		100.0

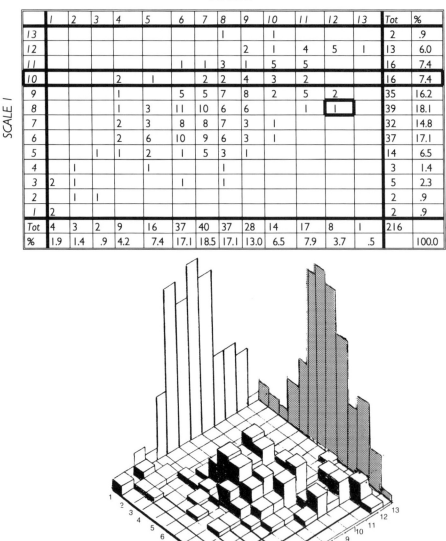

Figure 2.4: Bivariate frequency distribution

The figure shows a bivariate frequency distribution for scores from 216 people on two scales (Scale 1 and Scale 2) from a mood assessment inventory. Each cell of the table shows the number of people obtaining a specific combination of Scale 1 and Scale 2 scores. For example, the box drawn around one of the cells shows that just one person obtained a score of 8 on Scale 1 and 12 on Scale 2.

The frequency distribution for Scale 1 (shown down the right-hand side of the grid) is the same as that shown in Figure 2.1. The three-dimensional histogram shows the overall histogram for both Scale 1 and Scale 2, together with the bivariate histogram. From that, univariate histograms could be drawn for any 'slice' taken either vertically or horizontally through the table. The horizontal slice for Scale 1 = 10 is highlighted on the table and analysed in Box 2.4.

Box 2.4

Distribution of scores on Scale 2 for people with Scale 1 score of 10
(Data represented as histogram – see below.)

Score S	frequency f	$S \times f$	$S^2 \times f$	
1	0			
2	0			
3	0			
4	2	8	32	
5	1	5	25	
6	0			
7	2	14	98	
8	2	16	128	Sample mean (7.49)
9	4	36	324	
10	3	30	300	
11	2	22	242	
12	0			
13	0			
Totals	6	131	1149	

For:	Scale 1 = 10 slice	Whole sample
Mean	8.19	7.49
Variance	5.10	5.41
SD	2.26	2.33
N	16	216

The mean for the slice = sum of the scores (131) divided by the number of
scores (16)
= 8.19

You can work out the variance and standard deviation (SD) using the technique
shown in Box 2.1.

Score(s)	1	2	3	4	5	6	7	8	9	10	11	12	13	Totals
Number of cases (F)	0	0	0	2	5	0	2	2	4	3	2	0	0	16
Score x Frequency	_	_	_	8	5	_	14	16	36	30	22	_	_	131
Score² x Frequency	_	_	_	32	25	_	98	128	324	300	242	_	_	1149

We can be a bit more specific. If we extract from the bivariate distribution the line of numbers, or 'slice', for a Scale 1 score of 10, we can see (Box 2.4) that the slice forms a univariate frequency distribution of its own. The mean of the slice is 8.19 and its SD is 2.26. Of the 16 people it contains, the majority (11) have scores above the mean for the whole sample. Without knowing anything about correlation coefficients, you could do worse than take the mean of this slice as your best prediction of John Smith's Scale 2 score. If you did, what sort of error might you make? Well, he could be any one of the 16 people in the slice we took, and hence the SD of the slice is your best estimate of the error you would be likely to make using the mean of the slice as your prediction of his score. Note that this SD is smaller than the SD of the whole distribution (which was 2.33). So, by using information about the relationship between the two variables, you can make a more accurate prediction of a person's score on one variable given that you know their score on the other.

THE BIVARIATE NORMAL DISTRIBUTION

The problem with working from the bivariate frequency distribution is that we are only looking at a relatively small sample of values drawn from what we assume to be two underlying normal distributions.

Whenever we obtain a sample of actual data, we draw those data from a much larger population of possible values. The mean and SD of the sample we draw provide us with estimates of the mean and SD of that much larger population of values. While our sample of data will never have a perfect normal distribution, we can generally assume that the population has. Similarly, when we obtain measures of correlation from a sample of data, what we are trying to estimate is the relationship between the variables in the population from which our sample was drawn.

While we always have to work with sample data, we are generally interested in what that sample data tells us about the population it was drawn from. In psychometrics this is true in two ways. First, when constructing a test to measure some specific trait, we sample items or questions from all the possible items we might construct to provide information about that trait. We are not interested primarily in people's answers to specific questions, but rather with how well their overall score estimates the 'amount' of the trait that they possess. The second sense in which we 'sample' relates to people themselves. When establishing norms for a new test, we draw a sample of people who are representative of some population and then use the distribution information from our sample as norms for other people drawn from the same population. Thus, in both the sampling of items and the sampling of people, we are using our sample data to provide estimates of the properties of the population from which the data were drawn.

Just as we regard a univariate frequency distribution as being drawn from a smooth normal distribution, so we can see a bivariate frequency distribution as having come from a three-dimensional 'bell-shape' distribution. Look again at the three-dimensional histogram in Figure 2.4. It has a sort of flattened bell shape – imagine a round bell being squashed in from each side until its cross-section was an ellipse. For the Scale 1 and Scale 2 data, the elliptical 'bell shape' has its long axis running from left (low scores on both scales) to right (high scores on both scales) of the figure.

If we stick with using normalized z-scores for measuring both of our variables, then we can simplify the way we represent the relationship between them. We know that the bivariate distribution will have a 'normal' three-dimensional bell shape: what we do not know is how squashed or elliptical it will be. So, take a further imaginary step with your squashed bell! Now imagine slicing through its elliptical cross-section at the point where the curve of the bell changes from being convex to concave (the point of inflection on the normal curve). We can now use that ellipse as a two-dimensional representation of what is really a three-dimensional distribution. Have a glance at Figures 2.5b to 2.5e: each of the ellipses in these figures represent bivariate normal distributions.

For the next stage of our discussion of correlation we shall be assuming that we have ideal normal distributions for each variable – in other words, we will be looking at the way the variables are related in the population from which the samples of data were drawn.

THE CORRELATION COEFFICIENT

Let us start by considering a perfect positive correlation between two variables called X and Y (we use X and Y as names to indicate that we are talking about pairs of variables in general, rather than any specific pair). As we have already seen, a perfect relationship only occurs when we can predict exactly what every person will obtain on Y when we know their score on X (and vice versa). What we have in this case is a bell-shaped bivariate distribution in which the bell is squashed completely flat – so that it has become two-dimensional like each of the univariate distributions. Taking a cross-section through it gives us a completely flattened ellipse: which is a straight line!

This situation is depicted in Figure 2.5a. Each axis represents units measured in z-scores, with the mean (zero) in the middle. As we are talking of a perfect correlation between X and Y, any person's combination of X and Y scores will be located somewhere on the diagonal line that runs from the bottom left to the top right of Figure 2.5a. If they score -2 on Y they must score -2 on X, if they score $+1.6578$ on X they must also score $+1.6578$ on Y. If this were not so then the relationship would not be a perfect positive one. So, for any point along the X scale we can find the point at which we 'cut' the diagonal, and then work across to the Y scale to find our predicted score (similarly, we could work from Y to X). The predictions of Y when $X = -1$, $X = 0$ and $X = +1$ have been drawn on the graph.

Suppose the relationship was a perfect negative one. Everything would be the same, apart from the fact that the diagonal would now run from top left to bottom right. So when X was -1, Y would be $+1$ and vice versa.

Notice how, regardless of whether we have a positive or negative relationship, when we move one SD unit along the X scale, our predicted values of Y move one SD along the Y scale.

The next figure (2.5b) represents a correlation of $+0.91$ between X and Y. Notice how the diagonal line has now become an 'ellipse', with its long axis going from bottom left to top right. Recall that this ellipse is really just a way of representing a flattened three-dimensional bell-shape distribution by drawing its cross-section. If we now look at trying to predict values of Y for different values of X, we see that each value of X defines a vertical

Figure 2.5: Bivariate distribution for scores on two variables

Each figure, a) to f), represents a 'scattergram' or bivariate distribution for scores on two variables, X and Y, with the axes marked in z-scores. In each case, vertical lines drawn up from $z_x = -1$, $z_x = 0$ and $z_x = +1$ define three 'slices' through the distribution. For each slice, the mid-point of the slice is the mean of the distribution of z_y values associated with that z_x value. For $z_x = 0$, the mean of the z_y values will always be zero. For $z_x = 1$, it will vary as a function of the degree of association between the two variables.
A line drawn through the three points (from mean z_y for $z_x = -1$ to mean z_y for $z_x = +1$) is the regression line for the prediction of Y from X.

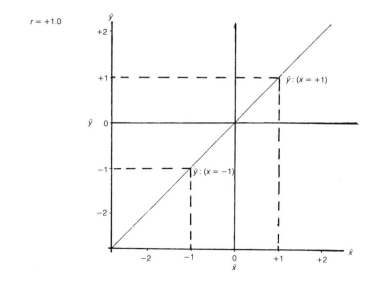

Figure 2.5(a)

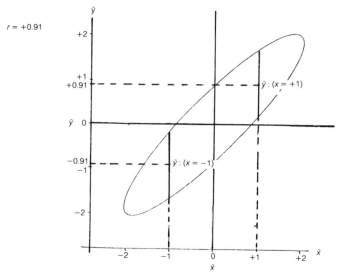

Figure 2.5(b)

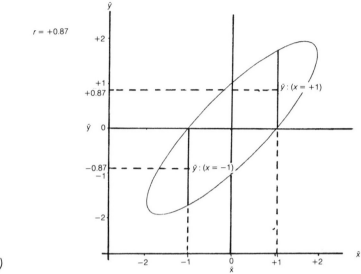

Figure 2.5(c)

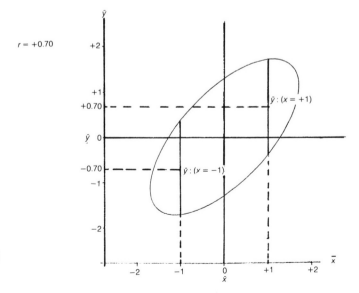

Figure 2.5(d)

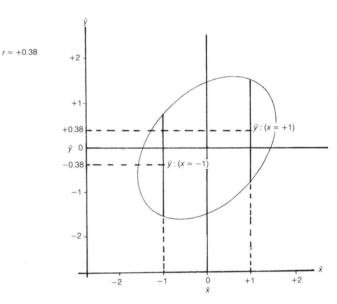

Figure 2.5(e)

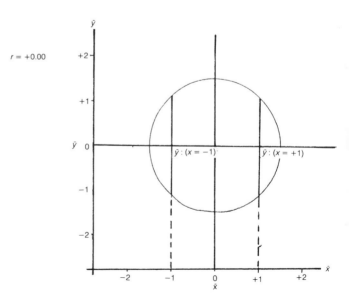

Figure 2.5(f)

'slice' through the bell-shaped bivariate distribution. Look back at the 'slice' we took in Figure 2.4 and Box 2.4: each vertical or horizontal line we draw through the ellipses in Figures 2.5 produces a univariate distribution of values of one variable for a fixed value of the other one.

For any such slice, if we want to predict values within it, our best predictor will be the mean of the slice. In the figure the mean of the slices taken at $X = +1$, $X = 0$ and $X = -1$ are shown. These must be our best predictors of what Y will be for these values of X. When we look at $X = +1$, we find that our predicted value of $Y = +0.91$, which is the correlation between X and Y. If you reverse this process and work from $Y = +1$ to X, you will find that the mean of the horizontal slice for $Y = +1$ corresponds to the point where $X = +0.91$. So long as we stick to using z-scores, the relationships between X and Y shown in this way are perfectly symmetrical.

Look at the remaining figures (2.5c to 2.5f) which show correlations of 0.87, 0.70, 0.38 and 0.00. As the correlation decreases, so the ellipses get 'fatter', and the relative length of each slice increases. When the correlation is zero, the bivariate distribution has a bell shape with a 'perfect' circular cross-section. Note how in this instance as we move from $X = 0$ to $X = +1$ or $X = -1$, the means of the slices through the distribution do not vary: they stay at $Y = 0$. So, whatever our value of X, our predicted value of Y is zero. Similarly, if we were predicting X from Y, we would find that whatever the value of Y, the mean of the horizontal slice would be: $X = 0$.

From looking at this sequence of figures, we can now define what a correlation coefficient is:

> The correlation coefficient (r) is the 'distance' (in z-scores) predicted scores will vary as a function of varying the predictor from z-score = 0 to z-score = +1.

The correlation coefficient is referred to by the letter r. Thus, the correlation between X and Y can be written:

$$r_{XY}$$

The letter r is used (rather than c for correlation), because the procedure we have been looking at derives from another, called 'regression' – hence the r. We will come back to regression very soon. We can now modify our argument which said that the mean was always the best predictor. If we know the correlation between X and Y (r), our best predictor of X is the z-score for Y multiplied by the correlation between X and Y (so long as X and Y are measured in z-scores).

More formally, we compute the predicted X score using:

$$\text{Predicted } z_X = r_{XY} \times \text{Actual } z_Y$$

Similarly, we can predict Y from X using:

$$\text{Predicted } z_y = r_{XY} \times \text{Actual } z_X$$

For example, if a person gets a z-score = 1.9 on X and the correlation between X and Y is 0.58, then we would predict their z-score on Y would be 1.102 (that is, 1.9 × 0.58 = 1.102).

Look back at the sequence of figures showing correlations from +1 through 0.91, 0.87, 0.70, 0.38 and 0.00. If you lay a ruler on each one and line it up with the means of the vertical slices for $z_X = -1$, $z_X = 0$ and $z_X = +1$, you will notice how the angle of the ruler rotates from 45 degrees when $r = +1$ to zero degrees when $r = 0.00$.

Another way of thinking about the correlation is that it defines the 'slope' of the ruler. When $r = 0.38$, then the angle of the ruler is such that for every one step you move to the right, you move 0.38 steps upwards. The lines are called 'regression lines' (we will later modify these definitions so that you can use raw scores rather than z-scores with them). The two equations given above are actually definitions of a straight line that has a 'slope' equal to the correlation.

REGRESSION TO THE MEAN

If we do not know the correlation between X and Y, our 'best guess' is that it is zero (as correlations are drawn from a theoretical distribution with a mean of zero). Hence, whenever the correlation between two variables is either unknown or known to be zero, it is best to predict unknown values as being equal to the mean. In all other cases, we can use the correlation coefficient to improve our level of prediction.

Remember, when we had no information about the correlation we had to use the mean as our 'best' predictor. That led to our errors of prediction having a variance equal to the sample (or more properly, the population) variance, while our predictions had zero variance (as they were all equal to the mean). Now, using the correlation coefficient, we saw how our predictions vary and hence have a variance greater than zero, while our errors of prediction are reduced and have a variance less than the total population variance.

So, as the correlation between two variables (X and Y) decreases (from either plus or minus one to zero), the variance of our predictions of Y from X (or vice versa) decreases, and that of our errors of prediction increases.

Figure 2.6 shows the predictions of Y made from X for $r = 0.70$ (using the equation: $z_Y = 0.70 \times z_X$). Notice how the predicted values are closer to the mean than the predictors. As the correlation between two variables decreases so the predictions made from one move closer and closer towards the mean of the other. This phenomenon is called 'regression to the mean'. In fact, when we are working in z-scores, the correlation coefficient is often called the regression coefficient (or more properly the 'least squares regression coefficient') and it defines the ratio of the predicted z-score to the predictor z-score.

Regression to the mean is important because it implies that although we know extreme scores on variable Y will actually occur, we will tend to underpredict them – as our predictions will always be rather closer to the mean than the scores we are trying to predict. Look at Figure 2.6: we know that about 95 per cent of all observations lie between +2.00 and −2.00 SDs. Yet we will predict 95 per cent of the scores on Y as falling between −1.40 and +1.40 SDs. There are other rationales we could use for making predictions. However, least-

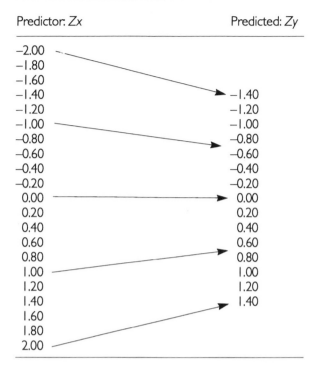

Figure 2.6: Prediction of Y from X for $r_{xy} = 0.70$

The arrows indicate the z_y values which would be predicted from given z_x values if
the correlation between x and y was 0.70. The fact that the range of predicted
values is 'squashed' closer to the mean than the predictors illustrates the phenomenon of 'regression to the mean'.

squares techniques are based on the assumption that we want overall to minimize the sum of squares of our errors of prediction. This 'conservative' strategy leads to the 'regression effect' in which we find an over-representation of
predicted values near the mean. The amount of regression increases as the
correlation between the variables decreases.

PARTITIONING VARIANCE: CORRELATION AND ALIENATION

Given a set of scores on variable X and the correlation between X and Y,
we can make a set of predictions: for each X score we can predict a Y
score. The total variance of the actual scores on Y can be divided up into
the variance of our predicted (Y') scores and the variance of our errors of
prediction:

Actual score on Y = Predicted score on Y + Error of prediction or $Y = Y' + (Y - Y')$

Variance of Y = Variance of predictions + Variance of the errors

We know already that the correlation is the distance in SD (z-score) units moved along the scale of the predicted variable when we move one SD unit along the scale of the predictor variable. We also know that a variance is the square of an SD. Therefore, the square of the correlation coefficient is the z-score variance of our predictions.

The total z-score variance of a variable, by definition, equals one. From what we have just said, the variance which variable X shares with, or has in common with, variable Y must be the square of the correlation between them:

Common variance $= r_{XY}^2$

The variance of the errors of prediction (that is, what is not shared with the other variable) must be one minus the square of the correlation (that is, all the variance which is left)

Residual variance $= 1 - r_{XY}^2$

In SD units this is:

$$\sqrt{(1 - r_{XY}^2)}$$

The total variance equals the shared or common variance plus the residual variance:

$$
\begin{aligned}
\text{Total variance} \quad &= 1 \\
&= r_{XY}^2 + (1 - r_{XY}^2) \\
&= r_{XY}^2 + k_{XY}^2)
\end{aligned}
$$

The coefficient k is called the coefficient of alienation and contains all the variance which is not shared (that is, the errors of prediction). This will tend to arise from two sources: error variance (from the fact that our measures are not perfectly reliable) and variance which is reliable but specific to one or the other variable. This distinction is a very important one and will be examined in more depth in the next chapter. However, when considering the prediction of one variable from another, both sources of 'unique' variance will 'alienate' the two variables – making it harder to use knowledge of one to predict the other.

The correlation coefficient is also sometimes called the coefficient of determination as it defines the extent to which, given one variable, we can 'determine' the other. As we have already seen, r is the SD of the predictions (in z-scores) which are made when we use least-squares regression as the basis for our predictions.

CORRELATION AS SHARED VARIANCE

So far we have been trying to understand correlation in terms of the 'shapes' of bivariate distributions. The concept of 'shared' or 'common' variance provides an alternative way of looking at things. We can consider a variable (for example, age or height) as describing variations along a single dimension. When two variables are perfectly correlated (that is, all their variance is common), then they are each describing variations which occur along the *same* dimension. When, on the other hand, they are uncorrelated ($r = 0.0$) they share no common variance, and changes in scores on one have no implications for the other. In this case, the measures relate to two dimensions which must be independent (that is, at right-angles to each other): the information that an object measures 59 cms along one of its axes is quite independent of what it might measure along its other two axes.

So if we consider each variable as varying in some specific direction (from low to high scores), then when two variables are perfectly correlated, they must be varying in exactly the same direction. If the correlation is positive, then as we move (in z-scores) along the measurement scale on one variable we must be moving an equal distance in the same direction along the measurement scale of the other.

We can represent this idea by drawing each variable as a line one unit long (representing one SD) pointing in a specific direction (which represents the direction of its variation from the mean to a z-score of plus one): such a line is called a 'vector' – as it has both a magnitude and a direction associated with it. For any pair of variables, these lines, or vectors, must meet at the point corresponding to their two means (where z-score = 0 in both cases) as, whenever someone obtains a mean score on variable X we always predict they will also obtain a mean score on variable Y – regardless of the size or direction of the correlation between X and Y.

So we have two lines, which meet at the point representing their two means. The angle between them represents the degree to which they vary in the same direction. Look at Figure 2.7. Here we can see a large positive correlation (a), an equally large negative correlation (b), a small positive correlation (c) and a correlation of zero.

We have seen that the correlation is a measure of the distance moved (in z-scores) along one variable when we move one z-score unit along the other. We have also seen that we can represent each variable as a 'vector' or line pointing in some direction. Finally, we know that the total variance of any variable can be divided into a part which it shares with another and the remainder (where the part it shares is the square of the correlation coefficient). Given all this, there has to be a very simple relationship between the correlation and the angle between our two vectors. The relationship is that the correlation is equal to the cosine of the angle and, conversely, the angle is the arc-cosine of the correlation. (This is explained in detail in Box 2.5. To follow the explanation, you will need to recall a bit of geometry and trigonometry from your school days.)

Do not worry if you are a bit rusty on the trigonometry. Basically, all we have to do is use a set of tables of cosines (or the COS function on a calculator or computer) to find the angle represented by any correlation. For any pair of variables, if we know the correlation between them, we can

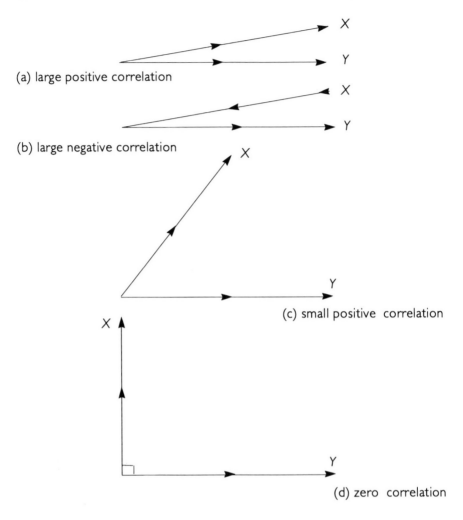

(a) large positive correlation

(b) large negative correlation

(c) small positive correlation

(d) zero correlation

Figure 2.7: Correlation between two variables by the angle between two lines

The figure illustrates the correlation between two variables by the angle between two lines. Each line is a 'vector' which represents the 'direction' in which the variable varies. For (a) and (b), the two vectors are separated by a small angle, indicating that much of their variance occurs along a common dimension. For (a) both vectors point in the same direction and hence the correlation is positive (that is, whenever one increases the other will tend to do so as well), while for (b) the vectors point in opposing directions indicating a negative correlation (that is, whenever one increases the other will tend to decrease). Figure 2.7(c) represents a much smaller positive correlation, as the angle between the two vectors is quite large.

Figure 2.7(d) represents a zero correlation: the two vectors are at right-angles to each other and so variation along any one of the axes does not entail variation along the other. Such variables are variously described as 'unrelated', 'independent', 'uncorrelated' or 'orthogonal'.

Box 2.5

Representing correlations as angles between vectors

Recall how the total variance in z-scores is the sum of two component squares:
  Variance of Y = Variance of predictions + variance of the errors of prediction
  Total variance $(1^2) = r_{xy}^2 + k_{xy}^2$
If you remember Pythagoras' Theorem, you will recall that for a right-angled triangle, the square on the hypotenuse (that is, the side facing the right-angle) is equal to the sum of the squares on the other two sides. Thus we can represent the relationships between r, k and the total variance by a right-angled triangle. If we do this (see Figure 2.8) it is apparent that the correlation (r) is the distance we move along one vector when we move one unit along the other (which corresponds to our original definition of the correlation).
What is more, we can see that the angle between the two vectors has a very simple relationship with the correlation. Using some basic trigonometry, in any right-angled triangle, the cosine of the angle (theta degrees) is defined as:
  cosine (theta) = (adjacent/hypotenuse)
As the side adjacent to the angle is r *(the* correlation) units long and the hypotenuse is one (the total SD) unit long,
  cosine (theta) = $r/1$
    $= r$
or   theta = arc-cosine (r)

---

draw the variables as two vectors meeting at an angle which is the arc-cosine of the correlation (see Figure 2.9).

This may seem somewhat academic at this stage, but it is important to realize that correlation is fundamentally concerned with the extent to which variables co-vary – either in the same or opposite directions. As such, it is useful to look at the relationship in these graphical terms where you can actually see how 'close' or 'far apart' the variables are, rather than as an abstract mathematical coefficient.

This becomes even more important if you have to deal with multivariate relationships and techniques such as factor analysis – that is, situations involving correlations between more than two variables – and situations involving correlations between actual measures and inferred ones (Chapter 3).

This way of representing correlation may also help in thinking about what a correlation has to tell you about two variables. People have a very natural tendency to confuse correlation with causation: that is, to assume that because two variables are correlated that changes in one cause changes in the other. This confusion is particularly likely to occur when we use correlation to make predictions about one variable from another – there is a strong tendency to assume that the 'predictor' causes the 'predicted'. All the correlation tells you is the extent to which scores on two variables vary in the same direction – that is, the extent to which they 'share' variance. This sharing can arise for a number of reasons:

the same direction – that is, the extent to which they 'share' variance. This sharing can arise for a number of reasons:

1. One variable may be a cause of the other (length of exposure to UV light and amount of sunburn).
2. They may interact – that is, each has causal effects on the other (for example, income and 'success').
3. They may both be the function of some other variable or set of variables (for instance, both calorie intake and weight may be the function of some set of underlying metabolic variables).
4. They may just be coincidental.

It is rare in human assessment to find correlations which result from simple causal relationships. The latter three conditions are far more usual. Indeed, the whole concept of psychological testing is based on the premise that the measures we obtain are the function of unmeasurable underlying traits. When we take a number of measures of some trait, we assume that the trait itself is the common dimension – the 'invisible vector' – along which all the measures share parts of their variance: to the extent to which

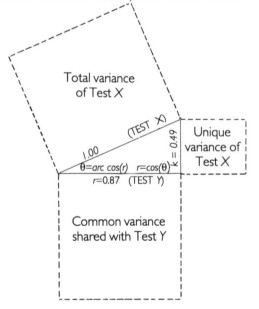

Figure 2.8: Correlation of 0.87 between variables X and Y

The figure represents a correlation of 0.87 between variables X and Y. The angle between the vectors is the arc cosine of the correlation between them. The total variance of each variable must be accounted for by the sum of its shared variance and its unique variance. This can be represented by the squares on the sides of a right-angled triangle. The hypotenuse represents the square root of the total variance of Test X. The second side is the distance moved along Y when one moves one SD unit along X (that is, the correlation, r=0.87). The third side is the separation or 'alienation' of Y from X (the SEe) and is the square root of the variance unique to Test X.

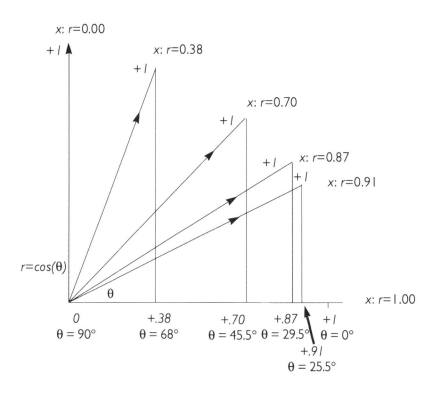

Figure 2.9: Correlations as pairs of vectors

The figure shows each of the correlations depicted in Figure 2.5a to 2.5f as pairs of vectors. As the correlation decreases from 1.00 to 0.00, so the angle – theta – increases from 0 degrees to 90 degrees. In each case, the distance moves along Y when one moves one unit along X is the correlation between X and Y.

ERRORS OF ESTIMATION AND CONFIDENCE LIMITS

If we know that someone's z-score on variable X is 1.3 and that the correlation between X and Y is 0.60, then that person's predicted z-score on Y would be 0.78 (that is, 1.3 multiplied by 0.6). The correlation, 0.60, is the SD of the predicted z-scores. What we also need to know, if we are to get some idea as to how accurate any particular prediction is likely to be, is the SD of our errors of prediction. This SD is given by the coefficient k: the 'alienation' of Y from X (see Figure 2.8). As it tells us how well we can estimate one variable from another, it is often referred to as the Standard Error of estimation (SEe).

If we are predicting scores on variable Y from scores on X, then the SE of estimation for Y from X (written as $SEe_{Y.X}$) is equal to the SD of Y multiplied by the coefficient of alienation. If we are using z-scores, the SD of both X and Y will be one.

So for z-scores:

$$SEe_{Y.X} = k_{XY}$$
$$= \sqrt{(1 - r_{XY}^2)}$$

and hence when we are dealing with z-scores:

$$SEe_{YX} = SEe_{XY}$$

For raw scores, we have to take account of the fact that this coefficient – like the correlation – is a proportion of one Standard Deviation. Thus we will need to multiply k by the raw score Standard Deviation to obtain our SEe for the raw scores.

Thus, the SEe for predictions of Y from X:

$$SEe_{Y.X} = S_Y \times k_{XY}$$
$$= S_Y \times \sqrt{(1 - r_{XY}^2)}$$

While the SEe for the predictions of X from Y:

$$SEe_{X.Y} = S_X \times k_{XY}$$
$$= S_X \times \sqrt{(1 - r_{XY}^2)}$$

Let us return to the example of someone with a z-score of 1.3 on X and there being a correlation between X and Y of 0.60. We predicted that person would have a z-score of 0.78 on Y. How accurate is that prediction?

$$SEe = \sqrt{(1 - 0.60^2)}$$
$$= 0.80$$

From the tables giving areas under the normal distribution curve (see Appendix), we know that 68 per cent of the distribution lies within one SD of the mean. Thus we can be 68 per cent confident that the person's score on Y would lie somewhere between: z-score $= (0.78 - 0.80)$ and z-score $= (0.78 + 0.80)$. That is, within the interval:

$$-0.02 < z\text{-score} < +1.58$$

If we did not use the correlation information, we would have had to guess that the score on Y would be at the mean (0) and that the SEe was simply the SD of Y (1). Hence our 68 per cent confidence limits would then have been:

$$-1 < z\text{-score} < +1$$

The importance of the SEe cannot be over-emphasized. Whenever we make predictions – either from one variable to another, or from some observed measure to some inferred underlying trait – our predictions have margins of error. We must always state the precision as well as the magnitude of our estimates.

Box 2.6 shows some example predictions of Y from a given value of X (a score of 20) for different levels of correlation between X and Y and different degrees of confidence. Note how the width of the confidence interval is a function both of how confident one wants to be and the degree of correlation between the two variables. Where the correlation is less than one, the degree of confidence you can place in the statement that the actual score on Y is *exactly* equal to the predicted score on Y is zero. At the other extreme, if you want to be 100 per cent confident about your prediction, then your confidence interval will have to stretch from minus to plus infinity. In effect this is saying that while we can be absolutely certain the actual score is somewhere along the scale, we cannot be at all certain about precisely where it is unless there is a perfect correlation between the variables.

MAKING ACTUAL PREDICTIONS – USING REGRESSION EQUATIONS

When using z-scores, the equations for predicting X (Z_X') from Y, or Y (Z_Y') from X, were very simple:

$$z_X' = r_{XY} \times z_Y$$
$$\text{and } z_Y' = r_{XY} \times z_X$$

We saw that these are really equations which specify the slopes of lines running through the means of the slices we took through the bivariate normal distribution. Unless the correlation between X and Y is one, there will always be two lines we can draw: one for the prediction of X from Y and the other for the prediction of Y from X. In each case we multiply the standardized deviation from the mean by the correlation to obtain the predicted value.

More generally, for the prediction of Y from X, the equation for this line can be defined as:

$$Y' = a_Y + b_{Y.X} \times (X) \text{ or } Y' = \bar{Y} + b_{Y.X} \times (X - \bar{X})$$

Where: a_Y = the 'intercept' of the line (that is, the value of Y we would predict when the predictor (X) equals zero);

$b_{Y.X}$ = the 'slope' of the line, and can be read as 'the slope of the function for predicting Y given X' (that is, the amount by which Y' will change every time X changes by one unit);

X = some particular score on the X scale.

$\bar{X}$ = the mean of X.

$\bar{Y}$ = the mean of Y.

Box 2.6(a)

Predicted values of Y from X

Predicted values of Y from X, where the raw score obtained on X is 20, given that the mean raw score for $\bar{Y}$ = 100 (with a standard deviation of 10) and the mean raw score for $\bar{X}$ = 15 (with a standard deviation of 5).

Correlation	Slope	Intercept	Predicted Y score (X = 20)
r_{XY}	$b_{YX} = (r_{XY} \times S_Y) / S_X$	$a_Y = 100 - b_{YX} \times 15$	$Y' = a_Y + b_{YX} \times X$
0.00	0.00	100.00	100.00
0.20	0.40	94.00	102.00
0.40	0.80	88.00	104.00
0.60	1.20	82.00	106.00
0.80	1.60	76.00	108.00
0.90	1.80	73.00	109.00
0.95	1.90	71.00	109.50
1.00	2.00	70.00	110.00

Alternatively, predicted values of Y can be calculated as follows:

$$Y' = \bar{Y} + b_{YX} (X - \bar{X})$$

Box 2.6(b)

Confidence intervals

Confidence intervals (from min. to max.) for each of the predicted values (Y') in Box 2.6. For 90%, the interval is +/-1.65 SEs; for 95%, the interval is +/-1.96 SEs; and for 99% the interval is +/-2.58 SEs.

	SE_{YX}			Confidence intervals					
				90%		95%		99%	
r_{XY}	$k=\sqrt{(1-r_{XY}^2)}$	$S_{YX}k$	Y'	min. – max.		min. – max.		min. – max.	
0.00	1.000	10.00	100.00	83.5	116.5	80.4	119.6	74.2	125.8
0.20	0.980	9.80	102.00	85.8	118.2	82.8	121.2	76.7	127.3
0.40	0.917	9.17	104.00	88.9	119.1	86.0	122.0	80.3	127.7
0.60	0.800	8.00	106.00	92.8	119.2	90.3	121.7	85.3	126.6
0.80	0.600	6.00	108.00	98.1	117.9	96.2	119.8	92.5	123.5
0.90	0.436	4.36	109.00	101.8	116.2	100.4	117.5	97.8	120.2
0.95	0.312	3.12	109.50	104.4	114.6	103.4	115.6	101.5	117.5
1.00	0.000	0.00	110.00	110.0	110.0	110.0	110.0	110.0	110.0

To obtain the predicted value of Y (Y') in raw score units, the slope is multiplied by the distance between X and the mean of X (in raw score units) and then the intercept is added.

The equation for predicting X from Y has exactly the same appearance, except that the slope will be different:

$$X' = a_X + b_{X,Y} \times (Y - Y)$$

Figure 2.10 shows the same 0.70 correlation we looked at earlier, but with the addition of raw-score scales for each variable. Consider the slope first. As we move one SD along the X axis we move 0.7 SDs up the Y axis. Hence the slope of the line for predicting Y from X is given by:

$$b_{YX} = (r_{XY} \times S_Y) / S_X$$

where: S_Y = the standard deviation of Y,
           S_X = the standard deviation of X.

If we consider the prediction of X from Y, then as we move one SD along the Y axis we move 0.70 SD along the X axis and hence the slope will be:

$$b_{XY} = (r_{XY} \times S_X) / S_Y$$

So, given the correlation and the SDs for each variable, we can calculate the slope for either regression line (predicting X from Y or vice versa). What about the intercept? We saw this was the value we predict when the predictor is zero. We know that when X equals the mean for X, we would predict that Y should equal the mean for Y. Hence:

If $\overline{Y} = a_Y + b_{Y,X} \times \overline{X}$
then $a_Y = \overline{Y} - b_{Y,X} \times \overline{X}$

As we know the means for the two distributions and the slope, we could now calculate the intercept. With the slope and the intercept calculated, we are in a position to predict the scores on Y for any given raw score of X.

CALCULATING CORRELATION AND REGRESSION COEFFICIENTS

A great deal has been said in this chapter about what a correlation coefficient is and what it can tell us about the relationship between two variables. We have also considered in some detail the issue of using information about this relationship to predict values on one variable from known values on the other. For many readers, it will not be necessary to know how to calculate correlation and regression coefficients. However, for those who do, Boxes 2.7 and 2.8 should provide all the necessary information about the computational procedures. Note that Box 2.8 gives a 'direct' method of calculating the regression slope coefficient which avoids the need to work out the correlation first.

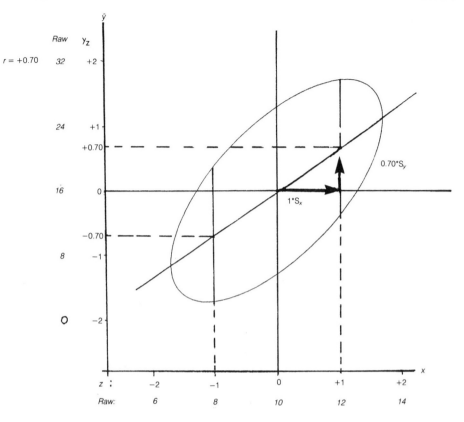

Figure 2.10: Raw scores plotted against Mean and Standard Deviation

The figure shows the same correlation of 0.70 as in Figure 2.5d. The raw score scales are marked on the axes showing that for Scale X the mean is 10 and the SD is 2, while for Scale Y, the mean is 16 and the SD is 8.

The regression line for predicting Y from X has been drawn in and the slope (or gradient) indicated. As X moves one SD to the right, Y moves 0.70 SDs up. In raw score terms, as X moves 2 units to the right, Y moves 0.70 times 8 units upwards.

Thus the slope is:

$$(r_{XY} \times S_Y)/(1 \times S_X)$$
$$= r_{XY} \times S_Y / S_X)$$
$$= 2.84$$

From this, we can find the intercept:

$$a = \bar{Y} - b \times \bar{X}$$
$$a = 16 - 2.84 \times 10$$
$$= -12.4$$

Thus the final regression equation is

$$Y' = X \times 2.84 - 12.4$$

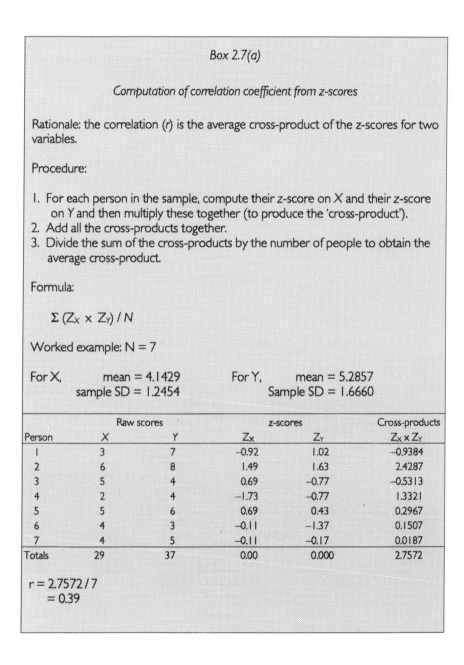

Box 2.7(a)

Computation of correlation coefficient from z-scores

Rationale: the correlation (r) is the average cross-product of the z-scores for two variables.

Procedure:

1. For each person in the sample, compute their z-score on X and their z-score on Y and then multiply these together (to produce the 'cross-product').
2. Add all the cross-products together.
3. Divide the sum of the cross-products by the number of people to obtain the average cross-product.

Formula:

$$\Sigma \, (Z_X \times Z_Y) \, / \, N$$

Worked example: N = 7

For X,   mean = 4.1429   For Y,   mean = 5.2857
         sample SD = 1.2454   Sample SD = 1.6660

Person	Raw scores X	Y	z-scores Z_X	Z_Y	Cross-products $Z_X \times Z_Y$
1	3	7	−0.92	1.02	−0.9384
2	6	8	1.49	1.63	2.4287
3	5	4	0.69	−0.77	−0.5313
4	2	4	−1.73	−0.77	1.3321
5	5	6	0.69	0.43	0.2967
6	4	3	−0.11	−1.37	0.1507
7	4	5	−0.11	−0.17	0.0187
Totals	29	37	0.00	0.000	2.7572

r = 2.7572 / 7
  = 0.39

Box 2.7(b)

Computation of correlation coefficient from raw scores

To avoid having to turn each value into a z-score before we can apply this procedure, the following procedure can be used on raw scores. This combines the conversion from raw to z-score and the computation of average cross-product into one equation. While it may look complicated, it is much more practical to use than the 'simple' formula.

Procedure:

1. For each person in the sample, compute the square of their score on X, the square of their score on Y and the product of their scores on X and Y.
2. Compute totals across all the subjects for the following: scores on X, the scores on Y, the squared scores on X, the squared scores on Y and the products of X and Y.
3. Enter the resulting values in the formula and compute the correlation coefficient.

Formula:

$$\frac{(\Sigma XY - (\Sigma X \times \Sigma Y)/N)}{\sqrt{(\Sigma X^2 - (\Sigma X)^2/N) \times (\Sigma Y^2 - (\Sigma Y)^2/N)}}$$

Worked example: $N = 7$

Person	X	Y	X^2	Y^2	XY
1	3	7	9	49	21
2	6	8	36	64	48
3	5	4	25	16	20
4	2	4	4	16	8
5	5	6	25	36	30
6	4	3	16	9	12
7	4	5	16	25	20
Totals	29	37	131	215	159
Mean	4.1429	5.2857			
Sample SD	1.2454	1.6660			

$r = (159 - (29 \times 37) / 7) / \sqrt{(131 - 29^2/7) \times (215 - 37^2/7)}$

$= 5.71429 / \sqrt{(10.85714) \times (19.42857)}$

$= 5.71429 / 14.52373$

$= 0.393$

Box 2.8

Computation of regression slope and intercept values

From the data given in Box 2.7(b).
For the prediction of Y from X:

Slope $b_{XY} = (r_{XY} \times S_Y) / S_X$

$$= \frac{(\Sigma XY - (\Sigma X \times \Sigma Y)/N)}{(\Sigma X^2 - (\Sigma X)^2/N)}$$

$$= (159 - (29 \times 37)/7) / (131 - 29^2/7)$$

$$= 5.71429 / 10.85714$$

$$= 0.526$$

Intercept – $a_Y = \overline{Y} - b_{YX} \times \overline{X}$
$= 5.286 - 0.526 \times 4.143$
$= 3107$

Hence, for any given X, the predicted value of Y (Y′) is given by
$Y' = 3.107 + 0.526 \times X$

For the prediction of X from Y:

$b_{XY} = (r_{XY} \times S_X) / S_Y$

$$= \frac{(\Sigma XY - (\Sigma X \times \Sigma Y)/N)}{(\Sigma Y^2 - (\Sigma Y)^2/N)}$$

$$= (159 - (29 \times 37)/7) / (215 - 37^2/7)$$

$$= 5.71429 / 19.42857$$

$$= 0.294$$

Intercept – $a_X = \overline{X} - b_{XY} \times \overline{Y}$
$= 4.143 - 0.294 \times 5.286$
$= 2.89$

Hence, for any given Y, the predicted value of X (X′) is given by
$X' = 2.589 + 0.294 \times Y$

Conclusions

In this chapter, we have looked in some depth at what a correlation is and its importance in predicting from one variable to another. We have seen how to compute a correlation coefficient and how to make raw-score predictions from one variable to another by developing regression equations.

When looking at the relationship between two variables, we must always keep in mind that the correlation coefficient can be used to tell us two things: how much variance the two variables share and how much is unique to each. Prediction or estimation of one variable from another always has two sides to it − how closely our predicted values co-vary with the actual values (as indicated by the correlation coefficient), and how variable are our errors of prediction (as indicated by the SE of estimation).

In the following chapters the importance of the need to keep these two aspects in mind will become evident as we see how correlation and regression are applied in practical psychometrics.

Reliability and Validity

3

David Bartram

The importance of reliability and validity has already been touched upon in earlier chapters. To be of any use, any measuring device (be it a ruler or a psychological test) should produce the same value or score if it is used to measure the same thing on two occasions. This assumes, of course, we are measuring something that is 'stable' (that is, something that does not change between the first and second measurement). The degree to which a measuring instrument achieves this repeatability is called its reliability. Quite simply, the more accurate a measuring instrument is as a device for measuring whatever it measures, the greater the degree of reliance we can put on the values it produces.

Validity is concerned with what is being measured, what the underlying characteristic is. When we ask about the validity of the test, we are asking 'What is it a test of?'. One of the scales of the *EPQ* (the *Eysenck Personality Questionnaire*: a widely used personality inventory) is claimed to measure extraversion. The extent to which this is true is a measure of the validity of the test.

It is important to note that validity is not an absolute property of a test: a test may be valid for one purpose (selecting craft apprentices) but not for another (diagnosing depression). A supposed general intelligence test may be rather better at measuring spatial ability than it is at measuring verbal ability. The *EPQ* may provide valid measures of extraversion but almost certainly does not provide valid measures of spatial ability. Reliability, on the other hand, is more an intrinsic property of the test and the way it has been constructed: the reliability of the *EPQ* does not determine what it may or may not be a measure of.

We will see later precisely what the relationship is between reliability and validity. In general terms though, reliability is a necessary but not sufficient condition for validity. In other words you can have reliable tests that have no validity, but you cannot have valid tests that are unreliable.

We will look first at reliability. Partly because of its importance – as the assessment of validity depends upon having reliable measures – and partly because the measurement of reliability raises some fundamental theoretical issues in Test Theory.

Test manuals can provide various sources of information about the reliability of test scale scores. These include data on the 'internal consistency' of the measure (the extent to which scores on each item are related to scores on other items), the stability of the measure across time (using correlations between successive administrations of the test) and measures of equivalence (where more than one form of the tests exists). These will all be described in detail later in the chapter. However, in order to understand why reliability is important and why it is measured the way it is, it will be necessary first to look at some theoretical issues.

Reliability

CLASSICAL TEST THEORY

The previous chapter discussed the idea that scores obtained on a test are a reflection of some underlying characteristic or trait. Classical Test Theory presents the simplest and most practical way of dealing with the problem of inferring a person's 'true' ability from an observed but fallible or error-prone measure.

The essential elements of the theory are that:

1. Individuals possess relatively stable traits.
2. Obtained (fallible) scores result from a true score and some error.
3. These errors are normally distributed about the true score and hence have a mean of zero (remember how deviations about a mean always sum to zero and hence have a mean of zero).

In other words, the score a person actually gets (X) is made up of their 'true' score (T) and the measurement error (e).

$$X = T + e$$

The true score has a 'fixed' value for a particular person at a particular point in time, while the error will have a value drawn randomly from a normal distribution with a mean of zero.

When we wanted to know a person's true height, we saw that the more measurements we took, the better their average was as an estimate of the true height. The SD of these measures provided us with a direct estimate of our measurement error. If the person really has a 'true' height, and if we were able to measure without error, then every measurement we took would give the same value – the true height. Thus the SE of the mean of the measures provides an estimate of how accurately the average of the obtained heights measured the true height.

So, for each person we measure, the score we obtain will contain some amount of error. If we measure a large number of people, then the following will be true.

1. The mean of their 'true scores' should approximate the mean of their 'measured scores' (as the measurement errors, being normally distributed with a mean of zero, will tend to cancel out).
2. While the mean of the errors or measurement will be zero, their variance will not. Indeed as the measurement process becomes less

'reliable' so the variance of the errors of measurement will increase. Thus, the variance of the true scores will be somewhat smaller than the variance of the measured scores – as the latter includes both true score variance and error variance:

Fallible score variance = True score variance + Error variance

$$S_X^2 = S_T^2 + S_e^2$$

The more accurately we can measure the underlying trait (height, anxiety, spatial ability or whatever) the less difference there will be between the variance of the true scores and that of the measured scores. Indeed, Classical Test Theory uses the ratio of these two variances to define the 'reliability' of a test:

$$\text{Reliability} = \frac{\text{'True score' variance}}{\text{'Fallible score' variance}}$$

Thus, we can define the reliability of a test as a measure of the accuracy with which it measures 'true' scores. Its theoretical maximum and minimum values are +1.0 and 0.0. Unfortunately, while this formal definition tells us what reliability is, it does not prescribe a practical method of assessing it. We can obtain the variance of the fallible scores, but not – directly – the variance of the true scores. What we have to do is find some way of estimating that variance. To see how this is derived, it is necessary to understand the Classical Test concept of 'parallel tests'.

PARALLEL TESTS

Later chapters deal in detail with test design and construction. For the moment, though, we can simply define a test as a collection of items; for example, questions to answer, statements to respond to, actions to carry out.

The notion of parallel tests is important, because it can be shown that the correlation between any pair of parallel tests provides an estimate of reliability. Strictly speaking, parallel tests are any series of operations that measure the *same* trait to the *same* degree. Suppose we had a test of 60 spatial ability items (all designed to measure the same trait). We could randomly divide the items up into 6 sets of 10 items each, or 3 sets of 20, or 20 sets of 3, and so on. In each case we would produce parallel tests if the sets of items had the following properties.

1. They should have the same means and these should equal the mean of the true scores.
2. They should have the same variances and these should equal the variance of the true scores plus error variance.
3. The correlation between any pair of them should be the same as that between any other pair.
4. They should all have the same correlations with any other variable.

These conditions are 'ideals' that in practice are never met. If we consider a number of parallel tests produced by sampling items from a large population of possible items, then we know that the means of each sample will vary, and that the SD of this variation will be the population SD divided by the square root of the number of items in each sample (that is, the SE of the mean – see Chapter 2).

STANDARD ERROR OF MEASUREMENT

It can be shown that where these conditions hold, the correlation between any pair of parallel tests is the reliability as defined earlier. Thus, the correlation between two parallel tests can be used as a measure of the accuracy with which each test measures true scores. By a bit of algebra, we can produce a formula which allows us to work out measurement error if we know the variance of the fallible scores and have an estimate of their reliability (see Box 3.1 for how this is derived). This is known as the *Standard Error of measurement* of the true scores:

$$SEm_X = S_X \times \sqrt{(1 - r_{XX})}$$

where: S_X is the SD of the scores for variable X.
               r_{XX} is the reliability.

In other words, when we use a fallible score as our best estimate of what a person's true score is, the SE of measurement (SEm) tells us how close we are likely to be to the true value. This is a very important equation. You should never regard the score a person gets on a test as being anything other than an estimate of their true score. Without knowing how good an estimate it is, it is meaningless. The reliability of the test tells you, indirectly, how accurate your measures are. However, the SEm provides a means of directly putting confidence limits round an obtained score. Box 3.1 gives some worked examples of confidence limits computed from the SEm. If this is your first read through the chapter, do not spend too much time looking at this now. When you have finished the chapter, it would be a good idea to come back and look again at the material in this Box and spend some time following some of the calculations through.

The mean, the Standard Deviation and the Standard Error of measurement are probably the three most important statistics to understand in psychometrics. The main reason we try to quantify the reliability of a test is to obtain an estimate of the SEm. Despite this, many test manuals fail to give SEm information. However, so long as estimates of reliability are available together with the SD of the raw scale scores, you can easily compute the SEm.

As defined above, the SEm indicates the amount of error made in estimating a true score from a fallible one. In the previous chapter, we examined the equation for the *Standard Error of estimate*, which has a rather similar form:

$$SEe_{Y.X} = S_Y \times \sqrt{(1 - r_{XY}^2)}$$

Box 3.1 (a)

Derivation of the formula for SE measurement from the definition of reliability

If the correlation between two parallel tests is r_{xx} :
1. the fallible score variance is S^2_x;
2. the error variance is S^2_e ;
and the true score variance is S^2_T;
then:

$$r_{xx} = S^2_T\ /\ S^2_x$$
$$r_{xx} = (S^2_x - S^2_e)\ /\ S^2_x$$
$$= 1 - (S^2_e\ /\ S^2_x)$$

If we rearrange this to get the error variance on the left, we have:

$$S^2_e = S^2_x \times (1 - r_{xx})$$

and hence the Standard Error of measurement can be derived as:

$$S_e = S_x \times \sqrt{(1 - r_{xx})}$$

Box 3.1 (b)

Example computation of SEm and confidence intervals

Raw scores:
Suppose John Smith obtains a raw score of 10 on Scale A of the Cattell 16PF. For the Cattell 16PF, Scale A has a mean of 19.20 and SD of 6.84 (general population norms). How confident can we be that his true score is below the mean ?

If the reliability of the scale is: $r_{xx} = 0.80$
   then the SE of measurement: $SEm = 6.84 \times \sqrt{(1 - 0.80)}$
                                             $= 3.06$

One SE either side of John's score gives the interval:
   $(10 - 3.06)$ to $(10 + 3.06)$
   6.94 to 13.06

As 68% of observations lie within one SD of the mean, then we can be 68% confident that John Smith's true score is between 7 and 13.

For 95% confidence limits, we use 1.96 SEms either side of the observed score:
   $(10 - 1.96 \times 3.06)$ to $(10 + 1.96 \times 3.06)$
   4 to 16

In fact John's score is just over 3 SEm away from the mean for the scale, so we can be at least 99% confident (see Appendix) that his true score is below the mean.

Box 3.1 (c)

Standard scores

For z-scores (which have an SD of 1), the SE of measurement is:

$$SEm_{z\text{-score}} = \sqrt{(1 - r_{xx})}$$

STEN and STANINE scores both have SDs of 2 and hence their SE of measurement will be:

$$SEm_{sten} = 2 \times \sqrt{(1 - r_{xx})}$$

$$SEm_{stanine} = 2 \times \sqrt{(1 - r_{xx})}$$

The following table gives z-score SEm and 95% interval values for a range of reliability coefficients.

To obtain STEN or STANINE intervals, multiply by 2.

To obtain raw score 95% intervals multiply by the raw score SD.

Reliability	Z-score SEm	95% interval +/- (1.96 x SEm)
0.50	0.707	1.37
0.60	0.632	1.24
0.70	0.548	1.07
0.80	0.447	0.89
0.90	0.316	0.62
0.95	0.224	0.44
0.97	0.173	0.34

This SE indicates the amount of error made in estimating the (fallible) score someone will get on one variable (Y) from a (fallible) score they obtained on another (X). If we wanted to use a person's current score to estimate the score they would get if they took the test again, we would calculate the SE of our prediction using this form of the equation:

$$SEe_{xx} = S_x \times \sqrt{(1 - r_{xx}^2)}$$

But, if we want to use their current score to estimate their true score we would calculate the SEm of our prediction using:

$$SEm_x = S_x \times \sqrt{(1 - r_{xx})}$$

The reason for the difference is that the SE of measurement is really the following SE of estimate:

$$SEe = S \times \sqrt{(1 - r_{XT}^2)}$$

where r_{XT} is the correlation between true and fallible scores and is sometimes referred to as the 'Index of Reliability'.

From our definitions of parallel tests we know that the correlation between any pair of parallel tests (that is, the reliability) is in fact the variance shared by the true and fallible scores. From the arguments presented in the previous chapter this means that the square-root of this variance must be the correlation between the true and fallible scores:

$$r_{XT} = \sqrt{r_{XX}}$$

Therefore $r_{XT}^2 = r_{XX}$

As we can get direct estimates of r_{XX} (from the correlation between parallel tests) we express the SE equation for estimating true from fallible scores in terms of r_{XX} instead of r_{XT}.

$$SEm_X = S_X \times \sqrt{(1 - r_{XX})}$$

THE RELIABILITY OF SUMS OF SCORES AND DIFFERENCES BETWEEN SCORES

Often when using assessment data, we want to combine scores from a number of different tests or subscales in order to get a single overall measure of someone's performance. We also frequently need to make comparisons between different people's scores on the same test (for example, to see who has done best) or a particular person's scores on the same test on different occasions (for example, to see if they have improved as the result of some form of treatment). Essentially, what we are doing in these cases is either adding scores together, or looking at the differences between them.

Before we can make these sorts of comparison (involving sums of scores or differences between scores) we will normally need to ensure that all the measures are on the same scale — for example, by converting all the raw scores onto a common standard score scale. Whether we need to convert the scores and whether it is sensible to combine them at all will of course depend on what the scores are and what we want to do with them.

Having produced a sum or a difference score, we need to know what its SE of measurement is — in order to know how much confidence we can place in it as an estimate of a true score. The derivation of the SEm for the sum or difference of two component scores is shown in Box 3.2.

For parallel tests (for example, the same test administered twice), the equations given in Box 3.2 can be simplified to:

$$SEm_{(X+X)} = SEm_{(X-X)} = 1.414 \times SEm_X$$

Box 3.2(a)

Sum and difference scores.

Derivation of the SEm

When we add pairs of raw scores (X and Y) together the variance of the resultant sums ($X + Y$) is:

$$SD_{(X+Y)}{}^2 = SD_X{}^2 + SD_Y{}^2 + (2 \times r_{XY} \times SD_X \times SD_Y)$$

for z-scores this simplified to: $(2 + 2 \times r_{XY})$

When we subtract pairs of raw scores (X and Y) the variance of the difference scores ($X - Y$) is:

$$SD_{(X-Y)}{}^2 = SD_X{}^2 + SD_Y{}^2 - (2 \times r_{XY} \times SD_X \times SD_Y)$$

for z-scores this simplifies to: $(2 - 2 \times r_{XY})$

Classical Test Theory tells us that the error components of scores on any two tests (or from the same test on two occasions) are independent of each other. If they vary independently of each other, the correlation between them must be zero. Thus, while the variances of the sum and differences scores will only be the same *if* there is no correlation between the component scores, the SEm for the total of two scores will always equal the SEm for the difference of the same two scores – regardless of the correlation between the component scores – as the last term in each of the above equations disappears when $r = 0$:

$$SE_{m(X+Y)}{}^2 = SE_{mX}{}^2 + SE_{mY}{}^2 + 0$$

$$SE_{m(X-Y)}{}^2 = SE_{mX}{}^2 + SE_{mY}{}^2 - 0$$

Thus the SEm for the sum of two scores is simply:

$$SE_{m(X+Y)} = \sqrt{(SE_{mX}{}^2 + SE_{mY}{}^2)}$$

and for the difference between two scores it is:

$$SE_{m(X-Y)} = \sqrt{(SE_{mX}{}^2 + SE_{mY}{}^2)}$$

Box 3.2b

Sum and difference scores

Reliabilities

The reliability of a difference score (for two scores X and Y) is given by:

$$r_{(diff)} = \frac{r_{XX} + r_{YY} - 2 \times r_{XY}}{2 - 2 \times r_{XY}}$$

The reliability of a sum (for two scores X and Y) is given by:

$$r_{(sum)} = \frac{r_{XX} + r_{YY} + 2 \times r_{XY}}{2 + 2 \times r_{XY}}$$

The following figures are for pairs of tests (X and Y), each with reliabilities of 0.80, but with varying inter-correlations (r_{XY}). Note that when the intercorrelation equals the reliabilities, the difference scores have zero reliability and the sum has maximum reliability. The reverse is the case for when the tests are independent (that is, $r_{XY} = 0$).

| | Reliabilities | | | |
r_{XY}	r_{XX}	r_{YY}	Sum	Difference
0.80	0.80	0.80	0.89	0.00
0.70	0.80	0.80	0.88	0.33
0.50	0.80	0.80	0.87	0.60
0.20	0.80	0.80	0.83	0.75
0.00	0.80	0.80	0.80	0.80

Differences between scores (whether two scores from the same person or from two different people) have to be treated with caution. The sort of situation where we might want to consider difference scores is where we have pre-tested somebody who then receives some form of treatment or intervention (for example, an assertiveness training course, or a series of psychotherapy sessions). After the 'treatment', the person is retested and we look at the difference between the before and after scores to see if they have 'improved'. The SEm for a difference score is exactly the same as that for a sum. However, as the correlation between the two component scores become increasingly positive, so the variance of the difference scores will decrease.

The implications of this are important. As the correlation between two measures increases up to the level of their reliabilities, so the reliability of the sum of their scores increases while that of the differences between their scores decreases towards zero.

THE RELATIONSHIP BETWEEN TEST LENGTH AND RELIABILITY

Let us return to the example of measuring someone's height. However many measures we take, the SD of the obtained values will represent our measurement error variance. Thus, this SD will always be the SE associated with using any single measure as an estimate of that individual's true height. However, as we increase the number of measures, the SE of the mean will decrease. In other words, the accuracy with which the mean of the measures represents the true height will increase. We have seen that the relationship between the number of measures taken (N) and the accuracy with which the mean of those measures estimates the 'true score' is given by:

$$SE = SD/\sqrt{(N)}$$

Test scores are always based on answers to a number of items. So, just as we get a more accurate estimate of a person's true height if we base it on the mean of a number of measures rather than on a single measure-ment, so we would expect to find that a test containing a large number of items will give a more accurate estimate of a person's true score than one that only has a few. If the items are from parallel tests, this is indeed true. In fact, if we know the reliability of a test with a given number of items we can also predict what its reliability would be if it contained any other number of items (either more or less) – assuming they are parallel.

This is done using a very famous equation: the Spearman–Brown 'prophecy formula', so-called after the two men who developed it.

$$r_{xx}' = \frac{(k \times r_{xx})}{(1 + (k-1) \times r_{xx})}$$

where: k is the ratio of the number of items in the new version of the test to the number in the current version,
          r_{xx} is the estimated reliability of the current version of the test,
          r_{xx}' is the 'prophesied' reliability of the new version.

As k gets larger and larger (that is, the new test gets longer and longer) so r_{xx}' gets closer and closer to one. This is as it should be: if we took all possible measures of some characteristic, their mean would have to equal the true score, as the sum of the measurement errors would be zero. Hence the reliability of a test containing all possible items (which could be an infinite number) would theoretically be one, whatever the reliability of any single measure.

Although we can, in theory, achieve any particular level of reliability by increasing the length of a test, in practice this is not feasible. People are not able to answer questions for hour after hour without getting tired and fed up. In effect, it is impractical for a very long test to satisfy the rule that it should be composed of parallel tests, both because the item writer would have difficulty generating the items in the first place and also because tired-ness, fatigue and loss of interest on the part of the test-taker will affect both the mean and the error variance. Even before we reach the limits where these sort of problems arise, we may find a test is too long.

In practical situations, there also tends to be a limit on the total time available for testing, and, within that limit, the need to obtain as much infor-mation as possible. In other words we frequently need to obtain quick but reliable measures of a large number of traits. Suppose we wanted to measure a range of 20 traits (say, 10 personality ones and 10 ability ones) and we had a total of two hours testing time per person available (in two 1-hour sessions). On average, taking administration time into account, we could allow about 5 minutes per trait. If any of the traits required tests taking 10 or 15 minutes in order to obtain reliable measures, we would be forced either to reduce the range of characteristics being measured, or have to find some very short test to compensate for the long ones.

It is often useful to use the Spearman–Brown formula to look at reliability in terms of test administration time. Box 3.3 shows the reliabilities for four (fictitious) tests, with the number of items they each contain and the time they take to administer. Tests C and D are the most reliable with approximately equal reliability coefficients. If we worked out the reliabilities for each test on the assumption that they each had 50 items, Test A (which has the lowest initial reliability) becomes the most reliable, with Tests B and C having approximately equal reliabilities. However, increasing the number of items to 50 would increase the time needed for Test A to nearly 3 hours! If we equate the tests for length in terms of time (say, 30 minutes each) then Test C will provide the most reliable measures.

Box 3.3

Reliability and test length

Relationships between test length (in terms of items and duration) and reliability (r_{xx}) (see text for explanation).

Test	Number of items	Standard form Duration (minutes)	r_{xx}	30-minute form r_{xx}	50 item form r_{xx}
A	10	35	0.68	0.65	0.91
B	30	20	0.79	0.85	0.86
C	45	25	0.88	0.90	0.89
D	100	45	0.87	0.82	0.77

WAYS OF MEASURING RELIABILITY

Test–Retest measures
We now have a good theoretical definition of reliability – as the correlation between parallel tests – and have seen how useful it can be as a means of estimating how accurate actual scores are (using the SEm). What we have not yet considered is how do we calculate reliability in practice?

The most obvious way of obtaining a correlation between two parallel tests is to give a sample of people exactly the same test on two occasions. The correlation between the two administrations of the same test is called *test–retest reliability*. The same test, repeated, must represent two parallel tests simply because the same items are used each time.

However, there are problems with this approach. While most traits are relatively stable, probably none is perfectly so. To obtain a retest reliability of 1.0, we would need both a perfect measuring instrument and a perfectly stable trait. As test–retest correlations will depend partly on the stability over time of the trait being measured, the correlation coefficient obtained is sometimes referred to as the *coefficient of stability*.

Typically, we find that for any given measure, the test–retest reliability will decrease with time. That is why it is important to note the time interval that has been used when interpreting retest reliability measures. Normally, unless we are looking at 'state' rather than 'trait' measures, we would expect to find high values, around 0.80 or 0.90 for periods of two or three weeks. However, these may frequently drop to 0.60 or less when the time interval is increased to a number of years (see Box 3.4). It can be argued (for example, Cattell *et al.*, 1970) that short- and long-term test–retest measures provide different information. The short-term measure (two weeks or less) is often referred to as a *coefficient of dependability*, as it indicates the extent to which one can depend on the instrument, given that the time interval is too short for there to have been any significant changes in the trait. For longer time intervals (two months or more) personality trait value may well show significant real changes in true score. Cattell uses the term *stability* to refer only to these longer term coefficients. Indeed it is argued that by subtracting the stability coefficient from the dependability measure one can obtain the fraction of variance due to real fluctuations in the trait.

Another problem with retest reliability, is that being exposed to the items on one occasion may affect how people respond on the retest – especially for ability tests and if the time interval is rather short. Even when people have not been told the results of their first session, there can be changes on the second occasion. Having done the test once, people have a general overview of all the items in the test – they know what is coming next, and which items they had difficulty with before. This may change the way they approach the test on the second occasion.

Finally, retest measures may tend to overestimate reliability. We have seen that the total variance of the fallible test scores is composed of 'true score' variance and 'error' variance. Some of the error variance will be random measurement error, while some of it will be variance which is neither true score variance, nor is it strictly error variance. It is systematic variance that is specific to the items being used. If we correlate a set of test items with themselves, the correlation will reflect both the true score variance and the residual item-specific variance.

While test–retest measures are useful and economical ways of providing estimates of stability across time, the actual coefficients obtained will always tend to over-estimate the 'classical' reliability of the test.

Alternate form reliability

An alternative to this approach is to construct two parallel 'versions' or 'forms' of the same test. Many tests exist in a number of forms – for example, there are forms A and B of the *EPI*, forms A, B, C and D of the Cattell 16PF and so on. Each form consists of a different set of items so that you can retest people without giving them the same questions or

Box 3.4

Retest and alternate form reliability

Example test–retest coefficients for different time intervals and equivalence coefficients for the first five scales (A to F) of the 16PF.

	Scale					
	A	B	C	E	F	
Equivalence						
Form A with Form B	0.57	0.49	0.54	0.52	0.61	n = 6476
Test–retest:						
Dependability – Short interval Form A maximum 2 weeks	0.86	0.79	0.82	0.83	0.90	n = 243
Stability – Long interval Form A males 4 years	0.49	0.28	0.45	0.47	0.48	n = 432
Trait fluctuation	0.37	0.51	0.37	0.36	0.42	

Source: Information extracted from Tables 2.1, 2.2 and 2.4 of Administrator's Manual for the 16 Personality Factor Questionnaire, Institute for Personality and Ability Testing, 1986: Champaign, Ill. IPAT.

statements to respond to. In this way you can obtain retest measures by giving people Form A of the test on one occasion and Form B on the next. When different forms of the same test are correlated, the estimate of reliability obtained is called *alternate form reliability* and the correlation is the *coefficient of equivalence.*

We can see from Box 3.4 that coefficients of equivalence tend to be smaller than stability coefficients – assuming they are measured over the same time interval. Note that these measures relate to the same test. If we correlate Form A with Form A we obtain a stability measure; if we correlate Form A with Form B we obtain an equivalence measure. The fact that one is smaller than the other does not mean that the 'reliability' of Form A has changed. In one sense a test does not 'have' a reliability. What analysis of retest and equivalence measures for different time intervals does is help to build up a picture of the relationship between the test, and the underlying trait and to tell us something about the stability over time of that trait.

Equivalence measures are attractive as they overcome the technical problem of confounding true score variance and item-specific variance. However, there is a cost. In practice, it is quite difficult to construct lots of different forms of the same test, as it necessitates trying to construct very large numbers of parallel items.

Split-half methods
There are a number of ways of assessing reliability without having to measure people on two separate occasions. We can take a single test administered on one occasion and treat the items as if they came from two parallel tests. If we had a test of 60 items, we could take the scores for the first 30 items and correlate them with the scores for the second 30. Alter-

---

Box 3.5

The Spearman–Brown prophecy formula

Use of Spearman–Brown prophecy formula to correct split-half reliability estimates.

For split-half measures, k, (the ratio of the new test length to the old test length) will always be equal to 2.
Hence:

$$r_{xx}' = \frac{2 \times r_{xx}}{(1 + r_{xx})}$$

where: r_{xx} is the correlation between the two halves of the text;
r_{xx}' is the estimated reliability of the full-length text..

Thus, if a split-half coefficient of $r_{xx} = 0.67$ was obtained, then the reliability of the text would be:

$$r_{xx}' = (2 \times 0.67) / (1 + 0.67)$$
$$= 1.34 / 1.67$$
$$= 0.80$$

---

natively, we could correlate the score for all the odd-numbered items with that for all the even-numbered ones. The correlation obtained is like the coefficient of equivalence described above, but with the items all presented on the same occasion. Indeed, if the correlation we obtain is good enough, we might decide to split the test for future use into two 'equivalent forms' each of 30 items.

This approach raises two problems:

1. The correlation will be for the reliability of a test which has only half as many items (30) as the whole test (60).
2. The correlation will vary, depending on how we split the items. If we had four items we would split them in three possible ways (1,2 – 3,4; 1,3 – 2,4 and 1,4 – 2,3). If we had 50 or 60 items then the number of different ways the items could be split into two equal-sized sets is a very large number!

The solution to the first of these problems has already been presented: the Spearman–Brown formula. If we split a test in half, and correlate the two halves, we can correct the obtained correlation using this formula (see Box 3.5) to see what it should be for a test twice as long as each half (that is, the original test).

Internal consistency
One way of looking at a split-half measure is that it tells us something about how consistent or homogeneous the items in the test are. If the items had low inter-item correlations, we would expect correlations between split halves of the test to be relatively low. On the other hand, if the

correlations between pairs of items were high, we would expect split-half reliabilities also to be high.

In fact the average of all the possible split-half correlations is closely related to the average of all the possible inter-item correlations. If we regard a test as comprising 'k' parallel items, find the mean of the inter-item correlations and then 'correct' this using the Spearman–Brown prophecy (with 'k' equal to the number of items in the test), we will obtain a coefficient that is equal to the average of the corrected correlations between all possible split halves. This is called the *coefficient of consistency*:

Internal consistency $= (k \times \bar{r})/(1 + (k - 1) \times \bar{r})$

(where $\bar{r} =$ the average inter-item correlation).

In fact we should be able to split a test into parts of any size – halves, thirds, quarters and so on, down to single items – then obtain an internal consistency estimate from the mean of the corrected inter-part correlations.

The Spearman–Brown formula is not really a practical way of doing this, though it does make clear the point that measures of internal consistency are a function of the variance that test items or parts of a test share with each other (that is, their average intercorrelation) and the number of items or parts.

A simpler way of calculating internal consistency is to use a formula based on the ratio of the sum of the individual item or part variances to the overall scale score variance. The general form of this equation is known as Cronbach's *alpha* (see Box 3.6 for a worked example):

$$r_{xx} = \frac{k}{(k-1)} \times [1 - (\Sigma S_i^2)/S_T^2]$$

The above equation is closely related to the Spearman–Brown formula, where k is the number of parts of a test, (ΣS_i^2) is the sum of the part variances and S_T^2 is the variance of the total test score.

The Classical Theory of strictly 'parallel tests' (whether these are single items or sets of items) makes the following assumptions:

1. the items measure a single factor or trait,
2. the item-intercorrelations are equal,
3. the items have equal variances,
4. the items have equal difficulties.

Like the Spearman–Brown equation, Cronbach's alpha assumes that at least the first three of these assumptions are valid. For other situations, a range of equations have been developed by Kuder and Richardson (1937). These are known as K–R 2, K–R 8, K–R 14, K–R 20 and K–R 21 and are used when either none (K–R 2), only the first (K–R 8), both the first two (K–R 14), the first three (K–R 20) or all four (K–R 21) of the assumptions are valid (see Box 3.6b for K–R 2 and K–R 14).

Cronbach's alpha coefficient is formally equivalent to K–R 20. The Kuder–Richardson equations are each presented in two forms. One uses item variances and the other is a modification designed to simplify computation for tests containing dichotomous (true/false or yes/no) items. For K–R 20, the alternative form is

$$r_{xx} = \frac{k}{(k-1)} \times [1 - (\Sigma pq_i)/S_T{}^2]$$

Where pq_i is the proportion of people responding 'Yes' to item i multiplied by the proportion responding 'No'.

If one or more of the assumptions described above are violated, then using the obtained coefficient will tend to underestimate the internal consistency. For the data shown in Box 3.6a, it can be seen that the assumption of equal item variances is not strictly true: if the internal consistency is

---

Box 3.6(a)

Internal consistency reliability: Computation of Cronbach's alpha from item variances and total scale score variance

Twelve people complete an inventory containing 10 items. For each item responses are made on a 6-point rating scale. The means and variances for each item are as follows:

Item	People 1	2	3	4	5	6	7	8	9	10	11	12	Item mean	Item SD	Item variance
1.	5	5	2	1	4	6	2	1	2	3	2	1	2.83	1.750	3.061
2.	4	4	3	3	6	3	4	3	1	3	4	2	3.33	1.231	1.515
3.	5	3	2	1	4	3	1	1	1	1	2	2	2.17	1.337	1.788
4.	5	6	4	5	6	6	4	5	2	5	5	3	4.67	1.231	1.515
5.	5	3	2	1	6	2	3	4	2	2	3	1	2.83	1.527	2.333
6.	4	1	2	2	4	5	2	2	1	2	2	1	2.33	1.303	1.697
7.	3	5	3	5	4	3	4	4	2	3	5	1	3.50	1.243	1.546
8.	5	4	1	2	6	6	3	3	1	3	2	1	3.08	1.832	3.356
9.	5	6	4	6	6	6	5	5	4	5	5	2	4.92	1.164	1.356
10.	5	2	3	2	5	5	4	2	1	2	1	1	2.75	1.602	2.568
Totals	46	39	26	28	51	45	32	30	17	29	31	15	32.41	14.220	20.735

The mean item-total scale score for the group is 32.41 and the variance of the scale scores (46, 39, 26... to 15) is 122.99.
Hence with $k = 10$ items, Cronbach's alpha measure of internal consistency is:

$= 10/9 \times [1 - 20.735/122.99]$
$= 10/9 \times 0.8314$
$= 0.924$

Box 3.6(b)

Internal consistency reliability

Computation of Cronbach's alpha using Analysis of Variance.

Repeated measures analysis of variance carried out on the same data used above gives the following summary table.

Source of variation	Sum of square	DF	Mean square
Between people	135.2917	11	12.2992
Within people	182.7000	108	1.6917
Between items	89.9083	9	9.9898
Residual	92.7917	99	.9373
Total	317.9917	119	2.6722

From this, Cronbach's alpha can be computed as:

$$= (MS_{between\ people} - MS_{residual}) / MS_{between\ people}$$
$$= (12.2992 - 0.9373) / 12.2992$$
$$= 0.924$$

---

worked out using the more appropriate K–R 14 equation, a slightly greater value of 0.926 is obtained (Box 3.6c).

FACTORS AFFECTING RELIABILITY COEFFICIENTS

We have looked at a number of different ways of computing reliability coefficients. For any given test, each of these will produce different values. The reasons for these differences lie in the fact that the various methods are not all equally affected by the same sources of unreliability.

Reliability can be affected by specific situational sources of error. These relate to variability in the way a test is presented and administered, the conditions under which it is carried out, and so on. Test–retest and equivalence measures of reliability can be affected by poor control and standardization of administration conditions. In addition, we have already discussed how these measures can be affected by lack of stability in the trait under consideration.

Measures of internal consistency, like all reliability estimates, should be interpreted with caution. If we asked people the same question 50 times and then looked at the internal consistency of our 'test' it would be very high. We would also expect it to have a high test–retest correlation (assuming the question related to some stable characteristic). However, it is obvious in this case that a high level of consistency would indicate a bad test. In striving for high reliability (as measured by internal consistency) the test constructor has to be careful not to fall into this trap: if you try constructing 50 items dealing, for example, with social extraversion you will find that it is very difficult not to start repeating yourself!

Box 3.6(c)

Internal consistency reliability: Kuder–Richardson internal consistency equations

K–R 2 for use when none of the parallel test assumptions is valid.
This can be used to find the reliability of an overall test battery score (where that is the unit-weighted sum of its constituent test scores). The reliability of each test has to be known (r_{ii}), as well as the variance of each text and the variance of the composite measure.

$$r_{xx} = (S^2_T - \Sigma S^2_i + \Sigma(r_{ii} \times S^2_i))/S^2_T$$

where: r_{xx} = the reliability of a battery of tests
                S^2_T = the variance of the total test score
                ΣS^2_i = the sum of the composite test score variances
                $\Sigma(r_{ii} \times S^2_i)$ = the sum of the products of the composite test score reliabilities and their variances.

K–R 14. For use when only assumptions 1 and 2 are valid (see text).

$$r_{xx} = [1 - (\Sigma S^2_i)/S^2_T] \times [(\Sigma S_i)^2/((\Sigma S_i)^2 - \Sigma S^2_i)]$$

where: r_{xx} = the reliability of a battery of tests
                S^2_T = the variance of the total test score
                ΣS^2_i = the sum of the item variances
                $(\Sigma S_i)^2$ = the squared sum of the item standard deviations.

For the data in Box 3.6(a):

$$r_{xx} = [1 - (20.735 / 122.99)] \times [14.22^2 / (14.22^2 - 20.735)]$$
$$= 0.8314 \times 1.1143$$
$$= 0.926$$

In general, the level of consistency we would expect of a test depends on the breadth of what we are trying to measure. If it is very specific (for example, the ability to carry out simple addition) we would expect internal consistency to be high, while if it is very general (mathematical ability) we would expect it to be lower.

RESTRICTION OF RANGE EFFECTS

As well as estimates of reliability being a reflection of the way items have been sampled for a test, they will also be affected by the way people have been sampled. Our original definition of reliability was in terms of the ratio of true score variance to fallible score variance. To get a 'good' estimate of reliability, then, we should sample people such that we are measuring the full range of levels of the trait we are concerned with. If we only looked at people with high levels of the trait, or only those with low levels of it, then our variance would be artificially restricted and the reliability would be underestimated. Where we know what the SD or variance of the fallible scores ought to be (an estimate of this would normally be in a test's manual), we can adjust the reliability using a *correction for restriction of range* formula (see Box 3.7 for details).

Box 3.7

Restriction of range effects on reliability

Correcting reliability estimates for restriction of range.

Assuming two samples of data (A and B) where we know the reliability of the data for sample B and the SDs for both A and B, the reliability for the sample A data will be:

$$r_{AA} = \{1 - [(S_B/S_A)^2 \times (1 - r_{BB})]\}$$

where: r_{AA} = the unknown reliability for one sample
S_A = the SD of that sample
r_{BB} = the known reliability for the other sample
S_B = the SD of that sample

Example:
A sample of 14-year-old school children is given a literacy test consisting of 45 items, and re-tested one month later. The raw scores are found to have a mean of 23 and standard deviation of 3.5. The reliability (test–retest with a one-month interval) of the test for this sample is 0.67. For a second sample of children, covering the full range of ability levels, a mean of 18 and a standard deviation of 5 is obtained on the same test. As the variance of the second sample is larger than that of the first (and the mean is lower), we can assume that the range of scores in the first sample was restricted and hence the reliability was affected by restriction of range. To correct for this

$$r_{AA} = 1 - ((3.5/5.0)^2 \times (1 - 0.67))$$
$$= 1 - (0.49 \times 0.33)$$
$$= 0.84$$

Validity

When a test is developed, the trait that it is designed to measure has to be defined in some way so that relevant operations (items or whatever) can be constructed. The initial definition specifies what the test is intended to measure. However, we cannot guarantee that the final product will actually measure what it was intended to measure. To accept, for example, that a new test *is* a test of 'spatial ability' we want more than an assertion from the test's author. In short we need to accumulate some evidence for the test's validity as an indicator of what it was designed to measure.

Validity is a rather less well-defined concept than reliability. The earlier definition of validity as being concerned with what it is that a test measures is rather too restricting. We may have very little idea as to what a test measures, and yet use it quite legitimately in job selection, because we have hard evidence that scores on the test are related to job success. It could be argued that this still satisfies the definition – as what the test measures, indirectly, is job success. However, rather than stretch the definition of validity, and restrict the idea of 'what a test measures' to the underlying trait that determines its scores, it would be better to elaborate the definition along the following lines:

> Validity relates to the appropriateness and justifiability of the things we say about scores on a test and the justification we have for making inferences from such scores to other measures.

The sorts of evidence used to 'justify' inferences vary from appeals to 'common sense' at one extreme to quantifiable empirical evidence at the other. There are really four major ways in which the term validity is used. In order of increasing quantifiability (and, some would argue, importance) these are face validity, content validity, construct validity and criterion-related validity. We will consider each in turn.

FACE VALIDITY

This refers to the degree to which the test-taker sees a test as being reasonable and appropriate for a given situation. For example, someone who has applied for training as a pilot will see tests of hand–eye co-ordination as being 'reasonable' while more abstract spatial ability tests will seem less appropriate.

Psychometrically, face validity is of little direct importance (except in so far as judgements of face validity by test-takers may correlate with other measures of validity). However, it has practical significance in aiding co-operation between the test-taker and the test administrator. People are more likely to take seriously activities which seem reasonable and which they feel they understand.

In practice, high face validity has no necessary relationship with what a test measures, nor how its scores may be justifiably used. However, it may have indirect effects by facilitating rapport between the test and the test-taker which may, in turn, increase reliability.

A related notion is that of *faith validity*. This refers to the strength of the test user's (as opposed to the test-taker's) belief in the validity of the test.

While it is natural for people to have their own preferences about which tests to use in particular situations, it is dangerous if these preferences are not firmly based on the psychometric data available about the tests.

CONTENT VALIDITY

The content validity of a test refers to the degree to which a test measures what it is supposed to measure judged on the appropriateness of the content. This may sound a bit like face validity. The difference is that face validity concerns the acceptability of a test to the test-taker, while content validity concerns the appropriateness of the content of the test as judged by 'professionals'. In practice there tends to be considerable overlap between these two notions of validity. Judgements about content validity are usually regarded as acceptable 'evidence' where the trait a test is supposed to measure can be very well defined (for example, ability to add two-digit numbers). In such cases, face validity will also be high.

The two may be distinguished, however, in that content validity concerns also the degree to which the content of the test covers the breadth of the trait being assessed. As we saw when discussing measures of internal consistency, we can make a test homogeneous by asking lots of very similar questions. Professional judgements of the items in relation to the defined aim of the test provides one way of seeing whether the range of items included is sufficiently heterogeneous for the trait they are meant to measure.

Of course, the fact that a group of experts agree that a particular test is a valid measure on the basis of its contents, is no guarantee that they are right. Really, such judgements are best seen as part of the process of test development – as an indication that we are on the right track. Mere opinion (whether expert or lay) is hardly evidence for validity.

CONSTRUCT VALIDITY

Many tests are constructed to measure traits that are hypothetical. 'Intelligence' does not exist in any physical or tangible form, nor does 'Extraversion' or 'spatial ability' or 'mechanical reasoning ability'. Yet we have created tests to measure all these physically non-existent qualities. Such qualities are called constructs as they have been constructed by us as a means of trying to explain and understand patterns of differences between people's behaviour. Because these constructs tend to be somewhat abstract and relate to aspects of a wide range of behaviours in a variety of situations, there is no one piece of real-world evidence that will, on its own, prove the construct validity of a test.

Construct validity is the closest we come to the idea of validity being whether a test 'measures what it is supposed to measure'. In practice, the construct validity of a test is gradually built up as more and more evidence accumulates about its properties.

For example, a new test designed as a measure of spatial ability should have positive correlations with other tests of spatial ability and it should correlate with real-world measures that are known to vary with differences in spatial ability (for example, navigation and hand–eye control tracking tasks). Also, it should not correlate with measures which are known to be independent of spatial ability. Good test manuals contain a range of detailed information about correlates of a test which help to provide an indication of what its measures mean.

The process of construct validation is never completed. The more a test is used and the more information accumulates about its relationships with other variables (either other test scores, or direct behavioural measures) the better defined becomes the construct it is measuring.

Building up construct validity involves two related procedures: *deductive validation* and *inductive validation*. The former assumes we start with a theory, which has helped define the content of the test and which will generate hypotheses about what should and should not correlate with test scores. Empirically testing such hypotheses is a process of deductive construct validation. Inductive validation assumes we start with a test measure and then try to infer what it must be a measure of by looking at its relationships with other things. In practice construct validation tends to involve both deductive and inductive steps. The balance between the two will depend on whether there is a well-specified theory underlying the original test construction process.

One particularly important technique used to establish construct validity is the analysis of a multi-trait, multi-method matrix (MTMM). In its simplest form, this requires two distinct traits or constructs (A and B) to be defined, and for there to be two distinct methods of measuring each one (for example, a situational task and a paper and pencil test). Examination of the correlations between the four possibilities that result from this can be used to provide both *convergent validity* and *divergent validity* for the two constructs.

The stipulation for convergent validity is that scores obtained from two different methods of measuring the same construct should correlate highly with each other. The stipulation for divergent validity is rather more demanding: the correlation between two different methods for measuring the same construct should not only be high, but must be substantially higher than that between two different constructs measured by the same method. This shows that the scores we obtain are primarily a function of the construct and not the method being used to measure them.

The analysis of an MTMM is not quite as straightforward as this sounds. In practice it can be difficult to define a range of methods for measuring each construct. Where multi-method approaches are used (for example, in assessment centres) the reliabilities of the methods may vary considerably and that of some of them may be unknown. As we will see shortly, this will affect the correlations obtained in the matrix, and hence the interpretation of it.

Ultimately construct validity relates to how well we know and understand what a test score means. This knowledge may be gained inductively or deductively. However gained in the first place, it should ultimately allow us to make practical predictions about real-world behaviour if the test is to be of any use.

CRITERION-RELATED VALIDITY

Some tests are designed to predict specific aspects of behaviour (for example, degree of success in a graduate job-training scheme, or number of therapy sessions required). Such measures of behaviour are generally referred to as 'criterion measures' or 'criterion scores'. Here the main concern is not so much with what underlying trait the test measures, but rather with how well it predicts the criterion. There is really no clear-cut distinction between criterion-related and construct validity. On the one hand, a test's construct validity provides the basis for making predictions as to what real-world criteria it should correlate with. On the other hand, real-world correlates of a test tell us something about what it is that the test measures – that is, its construct validity.

One of the most obvious areas in which criterion-related validity is important is personnel selection. For selecting new graduates into management training schemes, companies need to know if people without a 'track-record' have the ability to succeed. If they can produce operational definitions of what they mean by success, then it becomes possible to look at the relationships between measures of success (the *criterion*) and psychometric test scores (the *predictors*). For any given test, its correlation with a criterion measure is called a *validity coefficient*. Just as a test does not 'have' a construct validity, so it does not 'have' a criterion-related validity. It may have a high validity coefficient for one job and a low one for another.

Criterion-related validity is typically measured in either or both of two main ways: predictively and concurrently.

PREDICTIVE VALIDITY

As its name implies, this involves using scores from psychometric tests to predict future performance. The mechanics of a predictive validity study are roughly as follows. We administer the test (or tests) to a relevant sample of people (for example, applications for a job or entrants into a training scheme). We then wait until they reach the point at which criterion performance can be assessed (this may be anything from a few weeks to a few years later). The correlation between predictor (the test) and the criterion can then be calculated. Once this has been obtained we can, using a variety of statistical methods, make predictions about the likely criterion scores of future samples of people from the same population (that is, the job applicants or entrants to the training scheme).

This approach has a number of practical and technical problems associated with it. First, we may have to wait three or four years, before we can obtain the criterion measures: within many organizations, there will be economic pressures to make use of the test information before enough is known about its validity. Second, we have seen that reliability tends to decrease as we restrict the range of a measure.

With predictive validity studies we have a related problem of *attrition*. Assume that out of 500 applicants for a job, all of whom are given test A on a trial basis, 100 are subsequently selected and of these 70 remain in post three years later when criterion measures are obtained. The correlation between criterion and test scores for these 70 is almost certain to be subject to restriction of range effects both through selection and attrition – as neither of these are likely to be random processes. However, to use the test predictively, we want to know what the correlation would be between test and criterion at the point before selection occurs (that is, what it would have been if all 500 applicants had been selected and stayed for three years).

There are a number of useful equations which make it possible to make corrections for attrition and restriction effects. These correction procedures can get quite complicated (some examples of the equations which are used provide for reference in Box 3.8). Using such procedures we can obtain estimates of what the 'effective' predictive validity of a test at selection would be (see Box 3.8). However, as always in statistics, when we are using estimation procedures rather than direct calculations, we have to be cautious interpreting the results we get.

CONCURRENT VALIDITY

When the criterion and the predictor measures are obtained at the same time, the correlation between them is called the concurrent validity. Thus, if we administered an ability test to a sample of trainee apprentices at the end of their training course and correlated the test scores with their training assessments, we would have a measure of the concurrent validity of the test for apprentice training assessments. As such, concurrent validity is an important contributor to construct validity. Knowing what a test correlates with (apart from other tests) provides an important contribution to our understanding of what a test measures.

In practice, concurrent validity is often used as the basis for making inferences about the predictive validity of a test. Clearly, if one could base a new selection procedure on concurrent validity instead of predictive validity, one major drawback of the latter would be overcome: waiting for people to reach the point at which criterion scores become available. The procedure would be to administer the test to current job incumbents and correlate the test scores with the criterion measures. Then, if there is a correlation between test scores and criterion scores, it is argued that the former can be used as predictors of the latter.

While using assessments of concurrent validity as part of the process of building up a test's construct validity is perfectly acceptable, using it as a substitute for predictive validity is not. The problem of the time interval between selection and criterion assessment still remains, but in a different form. First, we have no way of estimating what the test score distribution should be for job applicants (this is the point we wish to predict from), hence we cannot make any corrections for selection and attrition effects. Second, the test is taken by people who may have been in a job for a number of years, or who may have just completed a training course. It is quite possible that their performance on the tests will have been affected by the experience they have had in the year(s) between their original selection and the present.

In short, concurrent validity should not be confused with predictive validity. It is quite possible for a test to have good concurrent validity and no predictive validity or vice versa.

Box 3.8(a)

Direct and incidental restriction effects

Formulae for explicit (direct) and incidental (indirect) restriction effects on validity coefficients with some worked examples.

Restriction of range due to explicit selection
Suppose that scores on Test X are used to select people for a job. Subsequently, the scores of those people who were selected are correlated with a job performance measure (Y). As people were explicitly selected with respect to X, we can estimate the predictive validity of the test in the applicant population using the following formula:

$$r_{XY}' = \frac{(r_{XY} \times (S_X'/S_X))}{\sqrt{[1 + r_{XY}^2 \times ((S_X'/S_X)^2 - 1)]}}$$

where: r_{XY}' = the estimated predictive validity for the applicant population,
            r_{XY} = the obtained predictive validity for the selected sample,
            S_X' = the SD of the test scores for the applicant population,
            S_X = the SD of the test scores for the selected sample.

Box 3.8(b)

Direct and Incidental restriction effects: restriction of range due to incidental selection

Suppose that scores on Test X are used to select people for a job. When applicants take Test X, they are also given a new 'experimental' test (Test Z). The scores on Test Z are ignored when people are selected. If there is a correlation between X and Z then any direct effects of restriction on X will have indirect effects on Z. Suppose that the scores on Z are correlated with the job performance measure (Y). As people were incidentally selected with respect to X, we can estimate the predictive validity of the test in the applicant population using the following formula:

$$r_{ZY}' = \frac{[r_{ZY} + r_{XY} \times r_{XZ} \times U]}{\sqrt{[(1 + r_{XY}^2 \times U) \times (1 + r_{XZ}^2 \times U)]}}$$

where: $U = ((S_X'/S_X)^2 - 1)$
            S_X' = the SD of the test scores for the applicant population,
            S_X = the SD of the test scores for the selected sample,
            r_{ZY}' = the estimated predictive validity of Test Z for the applicant population,
            r_{XY} = the obtained predictive validity of Test X for the selected sample,
            r_{ZY} = the obtained predictive validity of Test Z for the selected sample,
            r_{XZ} = the obtained correlation between Test X and Test Z for the selected sample.

Box 3.8(c)

Direct and incidental restriction effects: examples

Example:
A company uses Text A to select trainee graduates. Scores on the test have a SD = 5.68 for a sample of 500 applicants and SD = 3.56 for the 100 selected trainees. Subsequently it is found that the correlation between criterion scores on a training appraisal (C) and the Test A scores is 0.28.

What is the predictive validity of Test A, corrected for selection effects?

As Test A is the explicit selector, the adjusted validity will be:

$$r_{ac}' = \frac{(r_{ac} \times (S_a'/S_a))}{\sqrt{[1 + r_{ac}^2 \times ((S_a'/S_a)^2 - 1)]}}$$

$$= \frac{0.28 \times (5.68/3.56)}{\sqrt{1 + 0.28^2 \times ((5.68/3.56)^2 - 1)}}$$

$$= \frac{0.4467}{\sqrt{(1.1212)}}$$

$$= 0.4467 / 1.0589$$

A new test (Test B) is also administered to all the applicants, but the data are not used in the selection process. For the 100 selected trainees Test B had a correlation of 0.56 with Test A and a correlation of 0.33 with the appraisal criterion (C).

What is the predictive validity of Test B, corrected for selection effects?

As Test B is not the explicit selector, restriction of range will be due to incidental selection.

$$U = ((S_a'/S_a)^2 - 1)$$

$$= ((5.68/3.56)^2 - 1)$$

$$= 1.5456$$

$$r_{bc}' = \frac{[r_{bc} + r_{ab} \times r_{ac} \times U]}{\sqrt{[(1 + r_{ab}^2 \times U) \times (1 + r_{ac}^2 \times U)]}}$$

$$= \frac{0.33 + 0.56 \times 0.28 \times 1.546}{\sqrt{[(1 + 0.56^2 \times 1.546) \times (1 + 0.28^2 \times 1.546)]}}$$

$$= \frac{0.4868}{\sqrt{1.4847 \times 1.12118}}$$

$$= \frac{0.4868}{1.2901}$$

$$= 0.377$$

SYNTHETIC VALIDITY

One way round the problem of having to wait such a long time in order to assess the predictive validity of a test, is to use − at least as an interim measure − an estimate of synthetic validity.

While the size of correlations between predictor scores and criteria will obviously vary from test to test and from criterion to criterion, it has been found that by a careful examination of the criterion, one can make a very good guess as to which tests will and which will not predict it. In the occupational field, criteria tend to be measures of job performance, success or failure on a training course and so on. Analysis of the job or training course in terms of 'job components' can produce a specification for a battery of relevant tests. Given that we have information about the predictive validity of each test for performance on each job component, it is possible to construct what are known as *synthetic validities* for the prediction of performance on any new job.

The use of synthetic or job-component validity relies on what is referred to as *validity generalization*. Very simply, it has been shown that if a test is a good predictor of one particular job, it will also tend to be a good predictor of other similar types of job: the more similar the job, the greater the degree of generalization. For example, if we found that the correlation between a diagrammatic reasoning test and success on a particular engineering apprenticeship was 0.45, we would be justified in concluding that the test was a good predictor of performance on engineering apprenticeships. Additional information might enable us to generalize further: it may be that this test has correlations of between 0.40 and 0.50 with performance on a wide range of different apprenticeships.

What we see here is a process rather like construct validation. As we get to know more and more about what a test will and will not predict, so we are better able to judge in which new situations we should use it and in which we should not.

Relationships between Reliability and Validity

CORRECTIONS FOR ATTENUATION

It was argued earlier that reliability is a necessary but not sufficient condition for validity. Another way of saying this is that the reliabilities of two measures determine the upper limit on the correlation between those measures. Suppose we have two traits whose true scores are correlated with $r = 0.90$. We could only obtain a correlation of 0.90 between tests of those traits if our tests were perfectly reliable.

In Box 3.9 you can see how, from the Classical Test Theory definition of reliability, we can develop a formula that allows us to estimate the correlation between the true scores from the correlation between the fallible scores and their reliabilities. Look at the example in Box 3.9. From this we can conclude that if we had perfectly reliable measures of both variables, the correlation between them would be 0.58. This is useful for a number of reasons.

We have seen how the reliability of a measure can be increased − by increasing test length, and by reducing sources of error in the measurement procedure. Thus we can improve the correlation we obtain between any

Box 3.9

Correcting correlations for effects of attenuation

It can be shown that the variance shared by two 'fallible' measures, X and Y, is equal to the product of the covariance of their true scores and the covariance of each fallible measure with its true score:

$$r_{x_f y_f}^2 = r_{x_t y_t}^2 \times r_{x_t x_f}^2 \times r_{y_t y_f}^2$$

where: $r_{x_f y_f}$ = the correlation between the fallible scores on X and Y.
$r_{x_t y_t}$ = the correlation between the true scores on X and Y.
$r_{x_t x_f}$ = the correlation between true and fallible scores on X.
. $r_{y_t y_f}$ = the correlation between true and fallible scores on Y.

We know from our earlier discussion of reliability that the last two terms in this equation are estimated by the reliabilities of tests X and Y. Thus we can rewrite it as:

$$r_{x_f y_f}^2 = r_{x_t y_t}^2 \times r_{x_f x_f} \times r_{y_f y_f}$$

where: $r_{x_f x_f}$ = the reliability of text X.
$r_{y_f y_f}$ = the reliability of test Y.

What this shows is that the obtained correlation between any two variables will be reduced or 'attenuated' by the fact that neither is a perfectly reliable measure of the underlying true scores. What is more, the reliabilities tell us precisely how much attenuation will occur. Applying a bit of algebra to the previous formula results in the following one for the correlation between true scores on two variables:

$$r_{x_t y_t} = r_{x_f y_f} / \sqrt{(r_{x_f x_f} \times r_{y_f y_f})}$$

This is the ratio of the obtained correlation ($r_{x_f y_f}$) to the maximum attainable correlation given reliabilities of: $r_{x_f x_f}$ and $r_{y_f y_f}$.

From this we can see that the maximum correlation which can be obtained between any two fallible measures is the square root of the product of their reliabilities:

Upper limit on $r_{x_f y_f} = \sqrt{(r_{x_f x_f} \times r_{y_f y_f})}$

Example: Computing effects of attenuation on correlation coefficients.

A test with reliability of 0.80 is used to predict an instructor's ratings of apprentice work-pieces. Given the ratings have a reliability of 0.60 and the correlation between ratings and test scores is 0.40, what is the correlation between the true scores?

$$r_{x_t y_t} = r_{x_f y_f} / \sqrt{(r_{x_f x_f} \times r_{y_f y_f})}$$

$$= 0.40 / \sqrt{(0.80 \times 0.60)}$$

$$= 0.577$$

If rating reliability increased to 0.85, what correlation would be obtained between the test and the ratings?

$$r_{x_f y_f} = r_{x_t y_t} \times \sqrt{(r_{x_f x_f} \times r_{y_f y_f})}$$

$$= 0.577 \times \sqrt{(0.80 \times 0.85)}$$

$$= 0.476$$

two measures by increasing the reliabilities of one or the other or both. This will not, of course, change the correlation between their true scores. The example in Box 3.9 shows what would happen to the obtained correlation between test and performance ratings if we improved the reliability of the rating procedure to 0.85. To see what effect this would have, we simply use 0.577 as our estimate of the true score correlation (which will be unaffected by changes in reliability) and substitute 0.577, 0.80 and 0.85 in the following equation:

$$r_{XfYf} = r_{XtYt} \times \sqrt{(r_{XfXf} \times r_{YfYf})}$$

where: X_f is the fallible score on variable X.
          Y_f is the fallible score on variable Y.
          X_t is the true score on variable X.
          Y_t is the true score on variable Y.

The answer, 0.476, is the predictive validity we would expect to obtain with our improved performance rating procedure. Given this information, we would have to judge whether the cost of improving the reliability of the rating procedure was more than balanced by the savings obtainable from increasing the predictive validity from 0.40 to 0.476.

Overview

It may be evident by now that the distinction between validity and reliability is not really clear-cut. Technically, if we are looking at correlations of a test with itself, or with some alternative form of itself, then we are assessing reliability. If we are looking at the correlation between a test and some other measure, we are dealing with validity.

Consider two forms (A and B) of ability test X and two forms (A and B) of ability test Y. Let us also assume that these have both been designed as measures of the same trait. We label the correlation between XA and XB a measure of reliability, while that between XA and YA we would call a measure of construct validity. Yet we could equally look at the XA YA correlation as a measure of reliability, and the XA XB one as a measure of construct validity. Returning to the idea of convergent and divergent validity, what we have here are four methods of measuring the same trait. We would therefore expect the correlations between them to be high – the more similar the methods, the higher the correlations.

Other things being equal, we expect test–retest measures to produce high correlations which will tend to decrease as the time interval increases. These are likely to be higher than alternate form measures which in turn will tend to be higher than measures of association between two different methods of measuring the same trait. Such correlations will in turn tend to be larger than correlations between the tests and real-world criterion measures. The idea of validity generalization can be extended to include reliability. Indeed, one can look at reliability as a 'special case' of validity – the validity of a test as a predictor of itself. Necessarily this will limit the degree to which it might also act as a predictor of anything else. Alternatively, we can look at validity from the viewpoint of reliability: what reliance can we place in the score on test X as a measure of performance on task Y?

GENERALIZABILITY THEORY

This focuses on the issue of generalizing from what is known about a test to what is not known. There is not space in this chapter to go into this in any detail. However, in practical terms, all the procedures for measuring reliability and validity – which were derived from Classical Test Theory – still hold good. Generalizability theory provides a different way of looking at these and a way of being far more specific about what we mean when we talk of 'reliability' or 'validity'. Using analysis of variance techniques, test score variance can be analysed into components due to differences between people, items, administrations, forms, and so on. In addition, the interactions (that is, correlations) between these components can be examined.

A good understanding of reliability and validity is essential if one is to be able to make practical decisions about the appropriateness of a test for a particular purpose. In studying the test manual – and any other information that might be available – one has to ask whether the SEm is small enough to allow one to make the sort of distinctions between people that one wants to make. One needs to look at the evidence on validity and see whether the test really does provide the required measures.

In essence, information about test reliability and validity allows us to associate levels of confidence with the statements we make about test scores and what they imply. Without such information, test scores are simply uninterpretable numbers.

References

CATTELL, R.B., EBER, H.W. & TATSUOKA, M.M. (1970). *Handbook for the Sixteen Personality Factor Questionnaire (16PF)*. Champaign, Illinois: IPAT.

KUDER, J.F. & RICHARDSON, M.W. (1937). The theory of the estimation of test reliability. *Psychometrika, 2*, 151–160.

How Tests are Constructed

Paul Kline

In the last chapter we saw that tests must be both reliable and valid. In this chapter I shall describe how tests are constructed so that they possess both these characteristics, for it must be understood that sound test construction can ensure reliability, and to a lesser extent, validity.

Test construction is both an art and a science. The science lies in the techniques used for the selection and rejection of items, the art in the item-writing. In this chapter the concentration will be upon the techniques used in test construction, but some brief guidelines for the writing of adequate items will be given. I shall also describe how tests should be standardized so that they can be properly interpreted.

The emphasis will be upon the methods used to construct the majority of psychological tests of ability and personality, where the basic aim is to produce a homogeneous scale in which each item measures the same entity, for instance, anxiety. Certain other special methods are discussed in later chapters of this book.

There are two basic approaches to the construction of psychological tests. The first is the item analytic or factor-analytic method. The second is the criterion-keyed approach which was used in the development of the *Minnesota Multiphasic Personality Inventory* (the MMPI, Hathaway and McKinley, 1951), one of the most widely used personality tests.

In the first method the statistical analyses are aimed at the production of a monogeneous test that measures one dimension or factor. When such a set of items has been produced, it is always necessary to show what the set of items measures, that is, demonstrate its validity. This is by far the most commonly used approach to test construction, but it does mean that it is necessary to have a clear rationale for writing items. In the criterion-keyed method, however, items are written and are included in a scale if they can discriminate a criterion group from controls. Thus if we are trying to develop a scale to measure anxiety using the criterion-keyed method, items would be included if they could discriminate anxious subjects from controls. Intuitive notions of relevant items can be used.

There are two severe problems with the criterion-keyed method which limit its utility except in special circumstances. The first problem concerns the establishment of the criterion groups. This is usually no easy matter: for example, one might have difficulty when trying to differentiate between 'good' and 'bad' teachers; in abnormal psychology, as another illustration, there is poor agreement as to psychiatric diagnosis, thus making the selection of criterion groups dubious and unreliable. The second difficulty concerns the meaning of scales that are constructed by this method. It is often the case that criterion groups, even when they can be selected, differ on more than one variable. Schizophrenics might differ from controls on personality, occupation and ability, to take three important variables. This means that scales constructed from items that can identify these groups may be measuring a variety of variables. This makes interpretation of the scores difficult because a criterion-keyed scale might contain items relating to all of these. Consequently, even though it might discriminate, its meaning would be dubious.

From this it is clear that the criterion-keyed method is far from ideal. However, where it is required to select certain groups or screen individuals for certain purposes, this approach to test construction can be useful. For example, if a set of items was efficient at discriminating those who were unsuccessful in a particular training course, this test could be useful as a selection instrument.

The aim of the classical test construction method, as it is described by Nunnally (1978) is to produce a homogeneous test. The ideal procedure is to factor-analyse the test items and select those that load on the first factor. Factor analysis is a statistical method that can demonstrate the extent to which a test or item measures some underlying variable. However, there are considerable technical problems with the factor analysis of items and these have led test constructors to utilize a more simple approach – item analysis. I shall first describe the item analytic method and discuss its merits and disadvantages. I shall then describe how to construct factor analytic scales and suggest methods of overcoming the technical problems.

Item Analysis

The rationale of item analysis is simple. We aim to produce a homogeneous test. If a test is homogeneous, by definition, each item should measure the same variable. To investigate this, each item should be correlated with the total score on all items. This makes the assumption that the pool from which we are selecting our final test items is a reasonable sample of relevant ones. This assumption is not unfair since if it were violated we would be wasting time even trying to construct a test. The procedures for carrying out item analyses are set out below.

1. NUMBER OF ITEMS

Collect together at least twice as many items for item trials as are needed in the final test. Ideally even more items than this should be tried out. As was discussed in Chapter 3, scales with less than 10 items are unlikely to be reliable and 20 or 30 items per scale is a sensible target. Of course, the length of a test depends to some extent on its purpose and the population for whom it is designed. Sometimes, especially in the applied setting, tests have to be as brief as is consonant with reliability and validity. With young children and the very old, tests need to be short, particularly tests of ability. Certainly tests that take longer than half an hour to complete are burdensome and the subject may refuse to do them.

2. TRIAL SAMPLES

Try out the items on samples of subjects. It goes without saying, I hope, that the samples should resemble the population for whom the test is intended. This is particularly important for tests designed for specific groups such as psychiatric patients or children of a given age. Some examples will clarify this point.

The difficulty level of an item is an important criterion for retaining or rejecting it. Thus if we have an item such as 'Are you often really depressed?', this might be quite satisfactory for a normal non-psychiatric sample. If, however, we are interested in the personality characteristics of depressives, such an item would almost certainly fail to discriminate between depressives. The same problem arises with ability items such as are found in intelligence tests. An item designed for 10-year-old children would be rejected as too hard if we tested it in 5-year-olds and as too easy if we used it with 15-year-old children.

The size of the sample is also important. Item statistics tend to fluctuate from sample to sample. An item is essentially a one-item test and thus inherently unreliable (see Chapter 3). Certainly in item trials at least 100 items are desirable. The greater the number of items, the smaller the statistical error.

Another sampling variable that must be considered is the sex of the subject. In the field of ability it is generally the case that up to the age of 16 years, girls are superior in verbal ability, boys in numerical skills. Thus a combined sample could give misleading item statistics. Far better therefore, in this case, to have separate male and female samples. Whether separate samples are needed depends on the nature of the variable. However, in general it is sensible to have separate male and female samples. Items which show strong sex differences can then be abandoned.

However, there is a danger here and this must be discussed. It is not always generally realized that the distribution of scores on a test and sex differences are entirely item dependent. In the 1950s, to exemplify this point, there was a discussion in the *British Journal of Psychology* (for example, Lewis, 1957) as to whether intelligence was normally distributed or not. The recourse to test scores as evidence is perfectly fatuous since if harder items had been used, the scores would have been skewed, as they would if easy items were substituted. The same is true of sex differences. If items are selected on which girls do better than boys, girls will score higher. The reverse is equally obviously true. If there is no a priori reason to hypothesize sex differences on a variable then it makes sense to choose items that do not discriminate between males and females. It is usually better, therefore, to have separate samples of males and females and select items that behave the same in both groups.

In conclusion the practical procedure is to administer the items to two male samples and two female samples. Two of each allows for checking the reliability of the results.

3. ADMINISTERING THE TEST

When sufficient items and suitable samples have been chosen the items should be tried out. At this point it is usual to test the instructions to the test. All instructions should be clear and simple without the possibility, as far as is ever possible, of confusing subjects. The rule here is simplicity. After giving the test ask subjects whether they understood the instructions and check the tests to ensure that they have been filled in correctly. With adults, if more than five per cent are wrong, the instructions cannot be clear. With children a few more errors may be tolerated, but generally it is always possible to write instructions that are not misunderstood. Use short sentences and give examples.

4. THE ITEM ANALYSIS

For the simple item analysis two indices for each item are required: P, the proportion putting the keyed or correct response to each item; and r, the correlation of the item with the total score.

The proportion of the sample putting the correct response to each item is obviously simple to compute. Items to be retained in a test should have a P-value of between 0.20 and 0.80. Obviously if an item has a high correlation with the total score and its P-value is 0.19, just outside our limits, it would be quite reasonable to retain it.

These figures are not entirely arbitrary. The value of a good psychological test from the point of view of measurement is that it can be highly discriminating, compared with most other forms of assessment. Thus it is relatively easy to rate people for verbal ability, for example, into three categories, excellent, average and poor, with far more in the middle category than in the extremes. However, a good test can produce a huge range of scores. This ability to discriminate ultimately depends upon discriminating items. If an item is answered identically by all the sample, it is perfectly useless in that it has made no discriminations at all. Similarly, if only one subject out of 100 answered an item wrongly, this is the minimum discrimination possible. From this it is clear that items evenly split, that is, with a P of 0.50 are maximally discriminating. Thus in test construction we aim to have a large proportion of our items at this level of P.

However, it is obvious from this discussion that to have all our items with P values of about 0.5 would also be a serious error. In ability tests, where the point can be seen most clearly, very bright subjects would not be discriminated from each other with a test of items at the median P. They would all get them right. Similarly, low ability subjects would simply fail to score. That is the reason P values between 0.20 and 0.80 are advocated.

Factors such as these also demonstrate our previous point, namely, that the sample on whom the test items are tried out must closely resemble the population for whom the test is intended. If it does not, the P values could be quite misleading and the final test could turn out to be a very poor discriminator. For all these reasons, therefore, items should be selected for a test with P values between 0.20 and 0.80 that have been computed from a properly selected sample.

A satisfactory P value for an item is, however, not enough. It is a necessary but not sufficient condition for inclusion in the final test. The correlation with the total score must be high. In general the correlation should be greater than 0.3. As was indicated in my discussion of the P values, a high correlation (>0.6) should outweigh a minor infringement of the criteria for P values. What is really essential is the homogeneity of the test.

In many books on test construction (for example, Anstey, 1966) there is considerable discussion as to what is the ideal correlation coefficient to use for the item total correlation. I do not intend to enter this debate in any detail because with modern computing virtually anything is possible and many of the previous methods were ingenious short-cuts to lessen the terrible load of calculation. In addition to this in my experience of test construction, the difference in results from coefficient to coefficient are trivial psychologically and statistically. A good item is a good item.

In practice, therefore, all that is required is that the score on the item, however it is scaled, be correlated with the total score. For this the Pearson product moment correlation is the index to use. Most computer programs compute this coefficient. The point bi-serial correlation, as advocated below, is simply a numerical equivalent that is easier to compute on a calculating machine, or by hand.

The selection of the limit of the correlation with the total score is somewhat arbitrary. However, if it is remembered that the aim is to produce a homogeneous scale, it is obvious that the item total correlation should be as high as possible. Some readers might think that the limit of 0.3 was rather low for that means that only nine per cent of variance between item and total is in common. However, beware item total correlations that are really high, that is, >0.8. We would hope that the total score on a test measured a broader concept than any one item. Thus if items are correlating so highly with the total score it must mean (a) that the total score is very narrow and that (b) the items are themselves highly correlated.

Very high inter-item correlations are not good. Thus if two items had a correlation of +1, one of the items is quite redundant. If a set of items correlate beyond >0.8 with each other, each is adding in little new variance. They must be virtually identical items, paraphrases of each other and thus not useful. Again they would lead to the production of an exceedingly narrow test. That is why it is necessary to examine *test content* alongside these statistical indices. I shall discuss test content later in this section.

Actually the ideal in test construction is that each item correlates highly with the total but zero with the other items. This means that each item is adding an entirely new variance. In practice this is almost impossible to achieve but sometimes high test total correlations and *low* intercorrelations between items can be achieved. This will be briefly discussed later in this chapter.

One further point should be considered in relation to the item total correlation coefficient. This concerns the fact that the item itself has contributed to the total score, thus raising the correlation artificially. Although there are various correcting formulae for this the effect is negligible if a large number of items (say, 100) is tried out. If only 10 items are used a correcting formula is essential. The computation of the correction formula is set out in Box 4.1.

Having given the test to the samples of subjects, compute the point bi-serial correlation with the total for each item and the proportion putting the keyed response for each sample. Box 4.2 shows how item analysis can be calculated by hand without a computer in 8 simple steps.

Box 4.1

Formula for corrected item/total correlation

This formula is calculated on each item, particularly in cases in which there have only been a small set of items. The numerator is the item/total correlation multiplied by the standard deviation of the total scores of individual subjects on the test *minus* the standard deviation of the item being examined across all the subjects.

Formula 4.1:

One such is: $r_{it} \text{(corrected)} = \dfrac{r_{it}\,\sigma_t - \sigma_i}{\sqrt{\sigma_i^2 + \sigma_t^2 - 2\sigma_i\,\sigma_t\,r_{it}}}$

where r_{it} = correlation of item and total,
          σ_t = standard deviation of the total scores of test and
          σ_i = standard deviation of item.

---

5. SELECTION OF ITEMS AFTER FIRST ITEM ANALYSIS

This is done separately for the male samples and the female samples. I shall deal first with the male samples. Initially we select all items that meet the two criteria of $r = >0.3$ and P between 0.20 and 0.80 in both samples. If we are aiming at a 30-item test and we have 30 or more items all is well. If we have virtually 30 and need, say, two items it is sensible to select the two that come closest to meeting the criteria. If there is a real shortfall of items and all the rest are nowhere near the criteria, we can either rewrite some items (which I shall discuss below) or decide on a shorter test, if there is no reason for a longer one. However, a test of less than 20 items may well not be reliable, since reliability is related to length. This, however, is only the beginning of item selection. We now have to consider the content of the successful items and the possibility of some item rewriting. Items that differ markedly in the two samples are best left alone. If, however, an item passes in one sample and only just fails in the other, it could be included.

Obviously we want our final test to cover a certain segment of behaviour. In the case of verbal ability, for example, we would like our items to cover all its aspects – vocabulary, rhythm, assonance, verbal comprehension and so on. Thus, if our successful items covered all that was required, there is no problem. If, however, there was none from a certain category we would have to write some more of this kind and rewrite the ones that had failed. In the case of personality tests where a range of behaviours is sampled, as in extraversion, again it is important to ensure that successful items cover the whole gamut of behaviour. In personality tests it is all too easy to end up, after item analysis, with items that are little more than paraphrases of each other. In other words, a homogeneous test has been produced, but at the expense of validity. The test may be measuring a specific factor.

If a certain segment of what we want to measure has no successful items, then we write new items that we hope will cover that aspect of the test

---

Box 4.2

Computation of item analytic indices

1. Compute mean and standard deviation (σ) of whole group on the test.
2. For each item, compute the mean score on the test for subjects putting the keyed or correct response to that item (MH) and note the number of subjects who did this N(H).
3. For each item, compute the mean score on the test of those getting it right M(H).
4. For each item divide N(H) by N. This gives P – proportion passing each item.
5. For each item $1 - P = q$. This gives q.
6. For each item compute the mean score on the test of those getting it wrong (ML).
7. For each item multiply P by q. This gives Pq and take the square root.
8. The rP_{bis} for each item can then be computed using this formula:

$$rP_{bis} = \frac{M(H) - M(L)}{\sigma} \sqrt{Pq}$$

9. We now have rP_{bis} and P for items. In fact, there are many computer programs available for the computation of item analysis, and if there are many subjects and many items, it is sensible to use one of these programs.

---

and rewrite the old ones. Often the item analysis gives clues as to the cause of failure. Indeed usually these are so obvious (with the hindsight of the analysis) that it is embarrassing. I shall give a few examples from some of my own tests. This problem of item content and item rewriting is fully discussed in Kline (1986).

Example 1
I attempted to test tolerance to germs with the item 'Would you use someone else's toothbrush?'. This failed because too many subjects said 'No'. Clearly this was too disgusting for most people. Thus a milder version was used: 'Would you use a friend's toothbrush?'.

Example 2
In an item I asked whether the subjects' hobbies and interests were similar to those of most people. Few subjects claimed this was the case and the majority showed themselves to be uncertain about it. Clearly here the problem was the meaning of 'most people'. Who knows what most people do? I rewrote the item substituting 'many' for 'most', and the item was successful.

The reliability of the items (see Chapter 3) should be >0.7. Some test constructors, if the reliability falls below this figure add in new items – the next best according to the criteria – and then recompute the reliability until it reaches 0.7. However, this procedure is unlikely to be successful unless the extra items are quite good since the addition of poor items actually lowers reliability. Normally where we have 20 or 30 items which have reached the item analytic criteria, the alpha coefficient is unlikely to fall below 0.7.

So far all our procedures should have produced on this first item trial a homogeneous and reliable test for males. However, final cross-validation of the items is still required, as is validation of the test itself, and resolution of sex differences. We must now carry out all the procedures that I have described for the two male samples, for the two female samples. This should similarly result in a homogeneous and reliable test for females. Again cross-validation of these items is required and, of course, the resolution of sex differences.

We now have two tests — one consisting of items successful in the male population, the other of those in the female. One possibility is to leave it in this form and have two separate versions. These could be standardized in the two groups so that equivalent scores could be obtained from them. The practical disadvantage of this is that it is clumsy from the viewpoint of test administration to have two different forms. It also leads, inevitably, to the possibility of error in administration. This solution is not advised unless most of the items in the two tests are different. In my experience this is rarely the case. Thus this lazy solution is not recommended.

Usually it is found that there are relatively few disparate items. If so, it is possible to drop those which only worked in one of the samples and thus produce a scale suitable for use with both sexes. This is certainly the method which I would advocate. It is for this reason that a large pool of items is required in the first instance so that we have more successful items than we want to use, thus allowing us to drop those that only worked with one sex and to select for content among good items.

If it so happens that the successful items in the two groups are largely different, I would be suspicious as to what each test was measuring. It is perfectly possible to have genuine sex differences on a test using the same items. These would have different P values in the samples, but would still correlate highly with the total in each group.

In short, the best approach is to select for the final test items that have worked in both groups.

6. ITEM REWRITING AND CROSS-VALIDATION OF ITEMS

The great advantage of the item analysis procedures, which have been described, is that by examining the item analyses in two samples, the effects of item unreliability are eliminated. Effectively the items are cross-validated. However, even if no new items have to be added it is a useful final check if the test is given to one more sample for item analysis and the computation of the Cronbach's alpha (Cronbach, 1951), as in formula 4.2. Usually all items emerge successful. If one or two (but no more) are a little awry there is nothing to worry about. This final check is really to provide a set of indices independent of those which were the foundation of the test construction. It simply gives confidence that the previous procedures were correct. However, this cross-valuation is somewhat perfectionist and may be omitted.

If for reasons of content some items had to be rewritten these should be given, together with the full set to two samples so that the new items can be cross-validated. If these new items fail, it must be concluded that these aspects of the variable are not in fact components of it and they should be omitted. If they succeed they should be added to the final test.

7. THE FINAL TEST

The final test can now be drawn up. It consists of all the items which have passed all the item trials. The final item-analytic indices (P and r) should be recorded together with the alpha. This test is now ready for validation and standardization which will be described later in this chapter.

Advantages and Disadvantages of the Item-Analytic Method

This item-analytic method of test construction is capable of yielding excellent tests. It is a simple procedure, as can be seen, and tests thus constructed differ little from tests where other more complex methods have been used. There is, however, one problem with the method, which can occur although in practice it is fortunately rare. This concerns the concept of homogeneity.

It is possible for a test to be homogeneous yet measuring more than one dimension or factor, that is, not unifactorial. This can occur if the test measures two correlated factors, say verbal ability and intelligence. An item analysis could select items from both factors. Unifactorial tests are superior to others because the meaning of any score is always the same. On a unifactorial test a score X indicates the status of a subject on the factor. However, on a two factor test X can consist of any combination of two scores that would equal X. From this viewpoint a factor analytic method of test construction is superior because the fact that two factors loaded the test items would be revealed by the factor analysis. Nevertheless, in practice this is rare and as Barrett and Kline (1982) showed with the *Eysenck Personality Questionnaire (EPQ)*, item and factor analyses are virtually perfectly correlated.

In summary, for the construction of most tests the item analytic procedures that have been described are quite satisfactory. However, before I turn to the validation and standardization of tests, I shall discuss briefly some variants on the item-analytic method, factor-analytic methods and the criterion keyed procedure.

A simple variant of item analysis (which requires all the different samples) is to correlate each item with the total score and then compute alpha or KR–20 (Richardson and Kuder, 1939; see Chapter 3) for all items. The reliability will be low because of the poor items in the total pool. Then the worst item, by the criterion of the item total correlation is dropped, and alpha is recomputed. This process continues until alpha reaches its highest level. The items included at this point then constitute the test. Such a method guarantees high reliability, certainly the highest possible with the pool of items, and is virtually equivalent to the method which I have described in detail. If all the precautions of item content and replicability across samples and sexes are taken into account, there is little to choose between this and previous methods. This method has only become feasible with the advent of cheap and rapid computing. I prefer the standard item analysis because I can see the indices of each item and thus get some feeling about what is happening to the test. However, this is probably but a relic of a pre-computer age.

The Factor-Analytic Method

In principle the factor-analytic method is the best method for the construction of homogeneous and unifactorial tests. Indeed with huge resources for the development of items, testing of subjects and computing this is probably the recommended method. However, there are many technical and practical difficulties in the factor-analysis of items such that in practice the item-analytic procedures are preferable, as Nunnally (1978) has argued for reasons that I shall discuss below.

In principle, items are administered to samples (and there should be at least two of these to ensure replicability) and items are chosen which load on the general factor and have the requisite P-values. Indeed there are now two positive advantages with this method compared with item-analysis. First, there is no chance of accidentally having a bifactorial test. The factor structure of the items is revealed by the factor analysis. The second advantage stems from the fact that separate samples for males and females are not required since by inserting a variable, 1 for female, 0 for males, items that are affected by sex of subject can be seen. Such items will form a separate factor on which sex is the most salient variable.

These advantages are, however, offset by considerable problems. In a chapter of this length I cannot discuss these in detail, but I can summarize the main conclusions. For some detailed scrutiny of these difficulties readers are referred to Kline (1986). The first problem concerns the replicability of factor-analyses. With this technique there is an infinity of mathematically equivalent solutions. The way round this difficulty is to rotate the factors to simple structure. However, this requires that there be a large number of factors in the matrix. This, in turn, means that many tests have to be constructed together – which is not always feasible. Even if this can be done, a large number of items is needed. However, in factor analysis *at least* twice the number of subjects to items is required. In the end a huge matrix of item intercorrelators has to be factored, on a large number of subjects. This is a practical as well as technical difficulty for there is no consensus as to how simple structure can be reached. However, oblique *Direct Oblimin* rotation does seem to replicate factor structures. Simple structure as was defined by Thurstone (1947) refers to a set of factors which have each a few high loadings and the others zero or close to zero. In brief, a rotated factor analysis, where simple structure is obtained, is useful in the factor analysis of items. This in turn means that many items measuring a variety of factors, and at least twice as many subjects as items, are required. All this is difficult enough to achieve. However, there are yet further problems.

A serious difficulty with the factor analysis of items lies in item unreliability, a fact which has already been remarked. This is important in factor analysis where the factors attempt to fit mathematically and account for the correlations between items. This, therefore, leads to error. Fortunately the worst effects of these errors are counteracted by the fact that we have more than one sample. This eliminates the bad item which appears to be good, but it also eliminates the good item which appears to be bad. No empirical technique, however, can overcome this difficulty.

This source of error is compounded by yet another technical difficulty. This concerns the coefficient of correlation between the items. All of these are strongly affected by the item splits, which limit their maximum values and product moment correlations are not powerful with variables with less than 9 points. This statistical source of error means that the factors are often small. Sometimes in test construction the largest factor accounts only for 20 per cent of the variance. Usually phi is used with dichotomized items, despite these problems, but it must be realized that high loading items can be difficult to obtain.

There is a final difficulty in the factor analysis of items which is, perhaps, more a problem of interpretation than statistical artefact. Nevertheless, it is serious and it means that in inexperienced hands factor analysis can lead to quite dreadful tests. This is the problem of tautologous factors or, as they are referred to by Cattell (for example, 1957), 'bloated specifics'. If some of our items are little more than paraphrases of others, a factor analysis will produce just such a bloated specific with all the paraphrases and no others loading on it. Indeed a factor analysis of test items can produce a set of correlated factors on which only two or three items load, these being essentially all tautologous. This is particularly so when too many factors have been rotated – a common error especially when, as occurs in most statistical packages, factors with eigen values greater than 1 are rotated. As Kline has elsewhere argued (Kline, 1979) and Cattell (1978) has demonstrated, overestimation of significant factors leads to the breakdown of what can be thought of as the real factors underlying the items.

For all these reasons the factor analysis of items in test construction is only recommended where the test constructor is an experienced factor analyst who can confidently interpret different rotated solutions and who has considerable computing and research support.

Despite this it still remains the case that a factored test is theoretically superior, for reasons which I have already discussed, to an item-analytic test. For this reason a compromise is the best solution. I advocate, as does Nunnally (1978), that a test be constructed by the item analytic method and that the final version be factored. This will provide a check that the test is unifactorial. If it is not it is best to know and to form two scales, or if only a few items load on more than one factor these can be dropped. Generally, however, as I have indicated, there is a high correlation between factor and item-analytic indices.

The Construction of Criterion-Keyed Tests

I shall now describe how criterion-keyed tests are constructed. As with the item-analytic and factor-analytic methods, separate samples for males and females are required. Two each of these is also best to counteract the effects of item unreliability and other factors peculiar to any one sample. As with item and factor analysis, items are selected if they reach the necessary criteria in both samples and if there are no unwanted sex differences.

The rationale, logic, advantages and disadvantages of the criterion-keyed method have already been described so I shall begin immediately with the computational procedures.

CRITERION-KEYED TESTS: PROCEDURE

One method for establishing criterion groups is to take the top and bottom third on the test. Items are selected that will discriminate these groups. A more usual method is to set up the groups independent of the test. For example, if we were interested in the selection of accountants we would set up a criterion group of accountants and a group of controls matched for age, income and socio-economic class. Here items are selected that will discriminate these groups.

Another method is based on criterion scores. If, for example, we are attempting to select tank drivers we would obtain a rating of tank driving ability from instructors, or the marks in a tank driving test, and use this as a criterion score.

Generally, criterion-keyed tests are constructed by selecting items which will discriminate criterion groups, rather than from items which correlate with a criterion score. Sometimes if examination results are available, pass/fail criterion groups can be used.

The computation of the P values for the items is done by computing the proportion in both the criterion and the control groups who put the keyed response or the correct answer to each item. As I have indicated, 100 in the experimental and 100 in the control group, at least, is essential so that the P values may be reliable.

The next stage is the computation of Q between the group status and pass/fail on the item for each item.

This is the equivalent of the r for item analysis. If there is a criterion score, compute the correlation between each item and the score. Then select items which discriminate the groups or correlate significantly with the total score. Remember that for criterion-keyed tests there is no rationale for the items. We are interested solely in items which discriminate between the groups. It is unnecessary, therefore, to examine the content of the items. Examine the results in all samples and select items that meet the criterion – r >0.3 and P between 0.20 and 0.30 in both samples. Select the best 30 items.

If insufficient items meet the criteria either rewrite some items (as shown in our previous section) or opt for a shorter test but never below 10 items. These, of course, must be tried out on new samples. Then collect all successful items together and compute the alpha coefficient or the KR–20 reliability. This must be >0.7. As a final check, cross-validate the test on a sample of the criterion group and a group of controls. If this is satisfactory, a criterion-keyed test has been constructed. Box 4.3 sets out the procedures in the construction of criterion-keyed tests.

There is one final step in the construction of criterion-keyed tests which strictly comes under the heading of validity, but I shall deal with it here. I like to factor these tests, as a check. This is simply to indicate whether the test is unifactorial or not. This knowledge will affect interpretation of results, but we are now in the field of validity, a topic that I shall now discuss.

Validity

A test constructed by any of the methods that have been described will be reliable, in the sense of homogeneous, and if criterion-keyed, discriminating. It is not necessarily valid, and the next task is to demonstrate its validity. Since there are many different kinds of validity, I shall deal with each separately. By valid I mean a test which measures what it claims to measure.

While studies of the validity of the test are carried out it is convenient to compute the test–retest reliability. The higher this is the better the test, if all other things are equal. To obtain the test–retest reliability the test should be given to the same subjects twice, and the correlation should be computed. In a perfect world the test–retest reliability would be $+1$. Usually it falls below this but for ability tests it should be at least 0.9; for personality tests it is usually less than this, but 0.7 is a minimum figure. To avoid inflation of this reliability coefficient through subjects remembering their responses, the time gap should be at least three months. The sample size should be at least 100 subjects to avoid statistical error. If the test is devised for special groups, say schizophrenics, the test–retest reliability should be computed for these groups since it may differ, in these, from the test reliability among normal subjects.

A test is said to have face validity if it looks valid. It must be stressed that appearance can be deceptive, that face validity can be misleading. Note that the methods of test construction that have been described tend to produce (with the possible exception of the criterion-keyed method) face valid tests. Face validity is only important in as much as it is important for the cooperation of subjects. Adults are unwilling to give up time completing tests that seem absurd no matter how valid research may have shown them to be. One well-known test has items that always cause dissension: 'When you wake up, is your heart beating?' and 'Would you drink blood?'. A test should look at least sensible.

The concurrent validity of a test is demonstrated by its correlations with other similar measures. There is always the risk of some circularity here, since if there is a good test of the variable we are trying to measure, it brings into dispute the value of and need for a new test. If there is not, the value and meaning of correlations with a poor test is dubious. Sometimes, however, there is some sense in the procedure. For example, the best intelligence tests are individual tests that take about three-quarters of an hour to administer. If our new test measures intelligence with 20 items that take only 15 minutes to complete, it would be useful if valid. Thus a concurrent validity study with one of these tests, for example, the *Wechsler Intelligence Scale for Children (WISC)*, would be a good demonstration of its validity.

In many areas of measurement, however, no such benchmark tests exist and concurrent validity studies can never be definitive. At best they can constitute one piece of evidence relevant to the validity of the test.

Here the validity of the test is demonstrated by its ability to predict some criterion score or separate a group. For example, a test of neuroticism applied now should be able to discriminate between those who will need psychiatric treatment within the next year and those who will not. A follow up after a year would test its predictive validity. The old 11+ intelligence test showed some predictive validity in that high scorers achieved better 'O' level, 'A' level and degree classes than low scorers. The original

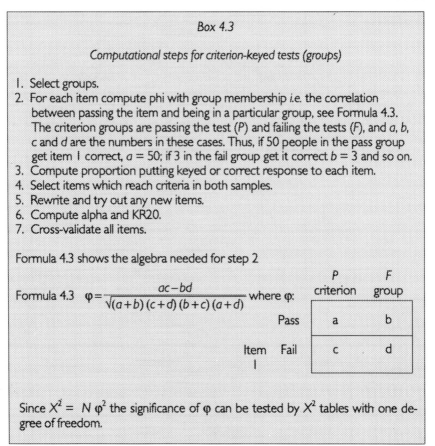

Box 4.3

Computational steps for criterion-keyed tests (groups)

1. Select groups.
2. For each item compute phi with group membership i.e. the correlation between passing the item and being in a particular group, see Formula 4.3. The criterion groups are passing the test (P) and failing the tests (F), and a, b, c and d are the numbers in these cases. Thus, if 50 people in the pass group get item 1 correct, a = 50; if 3 in the fail group get it correct b = 3 and so on.
3. Compute proportion putting keyed or correct response to each item.
4. Select items which reach criteria in both samples.
5. Rewrite and try out any new items.
6. Compute alpha and KR20.
7. Cross-validate all items.

Formula 4.3 shows the algebra needed for step 2

Formula 4.3 $\varphi = \dfrac{ac-bd}{\sqrt{(a+b)(c+d)(b+c)(a+d)}}$ where φ:

		P criterion	F group
Item	Pass	a	b
	Fail	c	d

Since $X^2 = N\varphi^2$ the significance of φ can be tested by X^2 tables with one degree of freedom.

Stanford–Binet test showed also impressive predictive validity in that those selected at five years of age as very bright had a most impressive record of adult achievement compared with controls (Terman, 1925).

The problem with predictive validity in validating a test lies in the difficulty with many test variables of knowing what to predict. For example a variable such as locus of control is extremely difficult, if predictive validity is desired.

In view of all these problems and difficulties with concurrent and predictive validity, many test constructors prefer to demonstrate the construct validity of their tests. Cronbach and Meehl (1955) introduced this notion of construct validity. This refers to the whole pattern of findings with the test which are interpreted in the light of the nature of the test variable. It thus includes predictive and concurrent validity. To demonstrate construct validity, we set out a series of results relevant to our test variable. I shall exemplify this by setting out the construct validity studies that might be undertaken for a new intelligence test.

1. It should correlate positively with other intelligence tests (concurrent validity).
2. It should correlate positively but low with other tests of ability.

3. It should not correlate with tests of personality or interest.
4. It should be correlated with academic achievement.
5. It should predict academic achievement (predictive validity).
6. It should be correlated with job success.
7. It should predict job success (predictive validity).

If a test met all these strict criteria, there can be little doubt that its construct validity as an intelligence test would be supported. One point is worthy of note, namely that it is often useful to demonstrate what a test does *not* measure. This is particularly true of pervasive variables that tend to emerge (often when we do not want them) such as intelligence or extraversion.

Another method of demonstrating the construct validity of a test, especially where it is difficult to set up studies of predictive validity, is to locate the test in factor space. This involves factoring the test with a huge variety of other tests including marker variables for the most clearly established factors. Kline and Cooper (1984) did this in a study of the validity of Cattell's *Objective Analytic Battery* (Cattell and Schuerger, 1978), an objective personality test. This test was factored together with the main ability and personality factors. Thus claims about the scales can be evaluated in the light of the factor loadings. Some scales loaded ability factors, others again clearly measured neuroticism. One set of tests measured the authoritarian factor. What was interesting was that these scales purportedly measured other variables.

It should be pointed out that this last method is good for ensuring that the two most common response sets in personality tests – social desirability and acquiescence – are not what our new test is measuring. This can be done by putting measures of both these response sets into the analysis. These should not have loadings on our test factor. This always needs to be done in the case of personality questionnaires since social desirability, the tendency to endorse items because it is socially desirable so to do, can distort validity as can acquiescence, the tendency to agree with an item regardless of content. In brief by using all or some of the methods discussed here, it is possible to demonstrate the validity of a test or at least find out what it does measure. Having established the validity of the test, it is now necessary to standardize it.

Standardizing the Test

All tests need to be standardized. This involves obtaining norms for the group or groups for whom the test is intended. Without norms the meaning of a score is impossible to interpret. Thus a score of 10 on a particular test of anxiety is very different in its psychological implications if we know that the mean of a normal population is 5 and that scores of 9 or more are restricted to those receiving psychiatric treatment, compared to the case where a score of 10 is the mean of the normal group.

The value of norms depends almost entirely on the adequacy of the sample from whom they are obtained. This sample must be large and representative of the population of which it is a sample. Indeed norms based upon poor samples can be highly misleading and are almost worse than no norms at all. There are, therefore, two crucial variables for samples: size and representativeness.

To eliminate simple statistical error a sample size of 500 is certainly sufficient. However, the representativeness of a sample is not independent of its size. For example, a sample of fire-eaters or sword-swallowers could be far less than 500. Indeed the total population may be less than this. However, a representative sample of adults would be far larger than 500. The difficulty really lies in being able to sample all the parameters of a population. The more heterogeneous the population the larger the sample must be. On the issue of representativeness, the Lorge–Thorndike Intelligence Test well illustrates how a population of children should be sampled.

Intelligence increases with age so that it is necessary to sample different age groups. Twelve age groups were used from 6 to 17 years of age. This is adequate, but ideal are three-monthly divisions, although this makes sampling truly complex. These authors used 11,000 children per age group so that their norms were free of statistical error. However, with a total sample of 136,000 children, the resources required are obviously enormous. To make this sample representative, a stratified sample of communities was taken. Communities were stratified by the factors known to be related to intelligence – adult literacy, proportion of professionals in the population, proportion of home owners, and the value of property. Communities were noted on these variables thus enabling a sample of communities to be drawn, all pupils at each age group in the sample of communities were then tested.

This is the ideal sampling procedure, but clearly it is beyond the scope of most test constructors. If a heterogeneous general population is to be sampled then by careful stratification a smaller but representative sample of around 5000 subjects can be drawn. Below this level norms begin to be shaky.

A possible way round the problem, and all depends upon the purpose of the test, is to develop special group norms. Anxiety neurotics, hysterics, school teachers (primary), school teachers (secondary), just for example. If a test is to be used for vocational guidance or selection, build up over time special relevant group norms: accountants, solicitors, barristers, general practitioners, and so on. Here stratified samples (taking the parameters relevant to the groups) should be used. A group of 300 subjects would be sufficient. If smaller groups have to be used potential users should be made aware that the norms could be misleading. For special groups, if due caution is shown smaller than perfect samples are probably better than having no norms at all. It should be pointed out that these huge samples are ideals. However, as in other areas of life, the closer we approach them, the better.

When the normative data has been collected, norms should be clearly set out. There are many methods for doing this, but I shall discuss only those that are most useful and generally employed by test constructors.

One method employs percentile ranks. The percentile rank of a score is defined by the percentage of subjects in the normative group who obtain a lower score. Thus, if a score of 75 is the 99 per cent level it means that 99 per cent of the normative group scored below this score. Percentiles are not recommended despite their simplicity, mainly because their distribution is such that minor differences around the mean are exaggerated and large differences at the tails of the distribution are minimized.

There can be no doubt that the best method of expressing norms is in *standard scores*. The great advantage of standard scores is that a standard score X always has the same meaning. Thus comparison of standard scores is simple. There are various types of standard score and these are described in Chapter 3.

The Test Manual

When a reliable, valid and standardized test has been produced all that remains is to write up the results into a manual. The test manual should be as brief as possible but should contain the following information.

1. A brief description of the test. What it measures, including a short discussion of the test variable, what the test is to be used for and the subjects for whom it is suited.
2. The rationale of the items, perhaps item by item, should be given.
3. The final item statistics should be given including the sample sizes, together with a brief account of the earlier item trials.
4. The alpha coefficient and test–retest reliability should be quoted, including details of the samples and of the time period of the test–retest reliability.
5. The validity studies should be reported. Correlations, factor loadings and discriminations between groups and all sample sizes should be given.
6. The norms should be clearly set out. Standard scores should be used and details of the samples, numbers and sampling methods should be given.

Some Final Points About Item Writing

In this chapter I have concentrated upon the statistical methods involved in the construction of psychological tests because these are common to all tests and are generally agreed upon by experienced psychometrists. Nevertheless, a test can be no better than its items (although if the psychometrics are bad, it can be considerably worse). Item writing is subjective and it is difficult to make generalizations as all depends upon the type of test and for whom it is designed. Most books, indeed, remain silent on this topic although Kline (1986) discusses items for all types of test in some detail. Nevertheless, some points are so important that I think they are worth including as a final addendum to the chapter.

1. In attainment tests of ability, where the content of items is crucial, have experts in the field, teachers for example, state what should be measured and then let them inspect the items.
2. Multiple choice items with five choices are a common and efficient item format. However, if the items are to be as good as they should be, it is essential that the distractors actually distract. Thus, if the choices, other than the correct response, are obviously wrong, the item becomes far too easy. This means that at some point the distrac-

tors in multiple choice items should be examined. It should be shown that each distractor is used and that good candidates are not attracted to the wrong answer. Actually, if this occurs the item fails the item analysis.

3. In writing personality questionnaire items, some simple rules will make the test more likely to be successful.

(a) Try to avoid items that are obviously socially desirable or undesirable. For example, few subjects would endorse an item such as 'I am usually quite untrustworthy' or 'I am a selfish person'.

(b) Try to make half the items keyed 'Yes' and half keyed 'No'. This does not overcome, but reduces the effects of acquiescence. The acquiescent individual is not confused with the high scorer; for example, if we are testing anxiety. The item 'Do you suddenly break into a sweat when faced with a difficult problem?' is keyed 'Yes'. Write an item to which the anxious individual will respond 'No' – 'I am at my best in examinations'.

(c) Write items as simply as possible, referring to behaviour rather than feelings. This leads to a more accurate response. 'I like sport' is far too vague. Better are items such as 'I play tennis at least once a month'; 'I play golf at least once a month'; 'I never watch sport on TV'; 'I never play football'.

(d) Try to avoid frequency terms such as 'usually' or 'often'.

(e) Make sure that each item contains only one point. 'I dislike competition' is fine, but 'I dislike competition and having to exert myself' is not a good item because either is possible on its own.

(f) Generally 'Yes'/'No' and 'True'/'False' items are best. Items with a middle category attract the uncertain and obsessional subject and are best avoided.

These are but the essentials of item writing. For more details readers should consult Kline (1986). Nevertheless if all these hints on item writing and the methods of test construction that I have described are followed, good tests can be constructed which turn out to be valid and reliable.

References

ANSTEY, E. (1966). *Psychological Tests*. London: Nelson.

BARRETT, P. & KLINE, P. (1982). The itemetric qualities of the EPQ – a reply to Helmes. *Journal of Personality and Individual Differences*, 3, 259–70.

CATTELL, R.B. (1957). *Personality and Motivation; Structure and Measurement*. New York: Yonkers.

CATTELL, R.B. (1978). *The Scientific Use of Factor Analysis*. New York: Plenum Press.

CATTELL, R.B. & SCHUERGER, J.A. (1978). *The Objective Analytic Test Battery*. Champaign, Illinois: IPAT.

CRONBACH, L.J. (1951). Coefficient alpha and the internal structure of tests. *Psychometrika*, 16, 297–334.

CRONBACH, L.J. & MEEHL, P.E. (1955). Construct validity in psychological tests. *Psychological Bulletin*, 52, 177–194.

HATHAWAY, S.R. & MCKINLEY, J.C. (1951). *The Minnesota Multiphasic Personality Inventory Manual* (Revised). New York: Psychological Corporation.

KLINE, P. (1979). *Psychometrics and Psychology*. London: Academic Press.

KLINE, P. (1986). *A Handbook of Test Construction*. London: Methuen.

KLINE, P. & COOPER, C. (1984). The construct validity of Cattell's Objective Analytic Battery. *Journal of Personality and Individual Differences, 5,* 323–347.

LEWIS, D.G. (1957). The normal distribution of intelligence: a critique. *British Journal of Psychology, 48,* 98–104.

NUNNALLY, J.O. (1978). *Psychometric Theory.* New York: McGraw-Hill.

RICHARDSON, M.W. & KUDER, G.F. (1939). The calculation of test reliability coefficients based on the method of rational equivalence. *Journal of Educational Psychology, 30,* 681–7.

TERMAN, L.M. (1925). *Genetic Studies of Genius.* Stanford, Calif.: Stanford University Press.

THURSTONE, L.L. (1947). *Multiple Factor Analysis: A Development and Expansion of Vectors of the Mind.* Chicago: University of Chicago Press.

Selecting the Best Test

5

Paul Kline

In our discussion of selecting the best test, it is necessary to be clear concerning the meaning of best in this context. First of all it must be realized that there is no one best test, no universal psychological instrument which will reveal all about our subjects. All depends upon the variable that we wish to measure, intelligence, verbal ability, extraversion or interest in helping people, just to mention variables that can be measured by well-known and respected psychological tests. Even when we are certain which variable we wish to measure, there may be no best test that we would always select. This is not because there are no good tests or because all tests are equally good. The point here is that the term 'best' has to be modified into best for a particular purpose, as Vernon (for example, 1950) always emphasized in his analysis of test validity. In other words in selecting a test we have to bear in mind not only the characteristics of the test (and here it must be said some tests, as we shall see, are unhelpful), but what we want the test to do. This certainly means that the characteristics of our intended subjects have to be carefully considered.

Nevertheless despite this caveat over the implications of the meaning of best, there are certain characteristics that a test must possess before we could consider its use.

The Essentials of a Usable Test

Most of the essential characteristics of a good test have been discussed in previous chapters so I shall not go into detail here about them. This will be a simple list.

RELIABILITY

All tests should be reliable in both senses of the word, that is, reliable over time and reliable in terms of internal consistency.

The internal consistency of the test should exceed 0.7. This coefficient should have been obtained from a sample of at least 100 subjects. If we desire to administer our test to a special sample of some kind, for example, people with learning difficulties, a disturbed psychiatric group, or managers, then its reliability among such subjects should be known.

There are various kinds of internal consistency reliability coefficient. The most accurate of these is coefficient alpha, mentioned previously, and ideally it is this index of reliability or its equivalent for dichotomous items, the KR–20, that should be quoted in the test manual. Nevertheless in practice other indices are satisfactory – split-half reliability or Hoyt's (1941) analysis of variance method.

Test–retest reliability is the correlation of the scores on a test given on two occasions. This should, obviously, be as high as possible and in an ideal world, it would be +1. However, the world is not ideal and tests are far from perfect so that in practice a lower limit of 0.7 is regarded as satisfactory. Certainly no test with a test–retest reliability lower than 0.7 should be used. Again this coefficient should have been computed on a sample of not less than 100 subjects and the time between testings should be between one and three months, to reduce the effects of subjects remembering how they answered the test items on the first occasion. Once again it is essential if we wish to use the test on a special group of subjects that we know the test is reliable in such a group. It is for this reason that we argue that the minimum figure for the reliability of a test should be 0.7. If the test is not to be used for individuals but for the discrimination of groups a lower reliability is perhaps permissible. However, if it is to be used for individuals, as in vocational guidance or selection, it is essential to minimize the standard error of score.

VALIDITY OF THE TEST

As has already been made clear, unlike reliability, there is no one validity coefficient. There are different types of validity and ideally we should like to see that the test which we select is valid on all criteria. However, with some kinds of tests, predictive validity for example is difficult to demonstrate. Nevertheless, some evidence for validity, other than face validity, must be presented in the test manual. Without such evidence a test should not be used.

To recap: test is face-valid if it appears to be measuring what it claims to measure. It is wise to choose a test with face validity simply to maintain good rapport with subjects. If a test *seems* nonsensical or irrelevant, no matter how good it is, many subjects will simply not try.

The concurrent validity of a test is apparent from its correlations with other similar tests. How high these correlations should be is a matter of judgement and all depends upon how good these other tests are. In the case of intelligence, extraversion and anxiety there are some good benchmark measures and for these variables concurrent validity is a good guide if the benchmark tests are involved. Generally where the criterion tests are less than perfect correlations greater than 0.4 provided that samples are large (greater than 100) would be satisfactory.

Predictive validity refers to the capacity of a test to predict relevant criteria. Since prediction in psychology is fraught with difficulty, largely due to the fact that so many different variables interact in the determination of behaviour (other than in the experimental laboratory) any sensible correlations greater than 0.3 would be acceptable, given, again, that samples were reasonable.

The construct validity of a test is supported by the whole pattern of results that has been achieved with it. This, therefore, embraces both concurrent and predictive validity together with other evidence such as what the test does not measure. To decide whether a test has or has not construct validity requires considerable judgement and experience and most test manuals make the best of their case. Generally if there is predictive and concurrent validity and if the test distinguishes groups in the way we would expect, it is fair to argue that it has construct validity. Where a whole pattern of results has to be considered the fact that individual correlations may be lower than desirable is not quite so important.

For some tests, especially of ability and aptitude, content validity should be expected. This refers to the coverage of items. In a test of mathematical ability, for example, it is essential that the items embrace all the relevant aspects of mathematics. Clearly content validity is important only in tests where what is to be measured can be clearly defined.

In brief, in respect of validity, any test that deserves use must have, in its manual, evidence for its validity, which can take any of the forms that have been discussed above. Nevertheless, while tests without evidence of validity should never be selected for use, there may well be valid tests that would still not be useful for many purposes; for example, in the case of an intelligence test if it were too difficult for all but leading scientists. A lesser-known criterion is that of the discriminatory power of a test. The computation of Ferguson's Delta, which is an index of this power is described in Box 5.1.

NORMS

Norms are the scores of groups on the test that enable meaningful comparisons of our subjects' score to be made and thus aid interpretation. For many purposes norms are essential. For example, in vocational guidance norms really are a *sine qua non*. If our client scores, say 8, on Cattell's factor G, conscientiousness, without norms little can be made of this score. On the other hand, if our task is to select from a large group of subjects who can best do a particular job as often occurs in the armed forces, and if we know that variables A and B are highly correlated with success in this job, norms are not important. In general, however, a test should have adequate norms. By adequate I mean norms for the general population computed on a good sample (at least 1000 subjects who form a representative sample), together with norms for any special groups to which the test is likely to be given.

Rasch scaled tests are the exception to this demand for good norms since these have a true zero score. However, few such scales have been constructed and Rasch scales are suited mainly to tests of attainment where zero has a real meaning. Furthermore, as Lord has pointed out (Lord, 1974) Rasch scales may be highly misleading (that is, their calibrations may be errorful) unless very large samples (more than 10,000 subjects) have been used in the calibration of the item weights.

This section can be easily summarized. In essence a test must be reliable, valid, discriminatory and possess norms based upon large and representative samples if it merits substantive use either in research or in the applied setting.

> ### Box 5.1
>
> #### Discriminatory power
>
> This is an index of the efficiency of a test that is rarely discussed. It refers, as the name suggests, to the capacity of a test to discriminate among subjects. Since one of the main advantages of psychometric tests, compared with rating scales and assessments by interview, is the fact that they are more discriminating, it obviously makes sense to choose a test that is maximally discriminating. However, I would only take this into account in text selection if all other things were equal. In fact, few manuals quote the index of discrimination. This is Ferguson's delta (Δ) (Ferguson, 1949). Ferguson's delta is at its maximum, one, in a rectangular distribution where equal numbers of subjects obtain each possible score, and 0 where there is no discrimination at all, that is, all subjects score the same.
>
> Formula 5.2: Ferguson's delta
>
> $$\Delta = \frac{(n+1)(N^2 - \Sigma F_i^{\,2})}{nN^2}$$
>
> where N = the number of subjects
>
> = the number of items
>
> and F_i = frequency at each score, that is, the number of subjects obtaining each score

Where Is Information About Tests To Be Found?

Even if it is agreed that there are important characteristics of tests, how do we discover whether a test is reliable or valid and so on? There are two sources of information. The first is the test manual. All test manuals should contain indices of reliability, validity and standardization data. These must include, if they are to be useful, details of the samples used in the studies, not only the numbers but also their provenance. A random sample of 200 sixth-formers from 10 schools constitutes a far better sample for normative purposes than 200 from one school. The second source of information of American and British Tests is to be found in the books that appear every five years and constitute a quinquennial bible for testers: *The Buros Mental Measurement Yearbooks* (for example, Buros, 1978). These contain all the details of tests abstracted from the manuals together with reviews by experts on the tests. In addition all references to papers and theses in which each test has been used are given. A good procedure is to scan the relevant section of Buros and then to send for the tests (and manuals) which seem possible.

As I have indicated at the beginning of this chapter, a test may be good for one purpose, but less suitable for another. To illustrate the different test requirements for different purposes I shall examine the requisites of tests for vocational guidance, for selection and finally for work with special groups. In so doing most of the major problems involved in the selection of tests can be scrutinized.

First, I shall discuss the selection of tests for vocational or educational guidance. Readers requiring more detail may be referred to Kline (1975).

Selection of Tests for Vocational Guidance

For whatever purpose we need tests, they should be reliable, valid, and discriminatory. An unreliable or invalid test is obviously worthless. However, for different purposes the emphasis on these characteristics differs so they will be briefly mentioned. Since we are making individual decisions, high reliability is essential. Choose the test (for the variable you are concerned with) that has the highest reliability. Again choose the test where discriminatory power (delta) is highest. A horizontal distribution produces the highest delta, but this is no disadvantage when we are dealing with individual cases.

For vocational guidance where we want as good a rapport with clients as is possible and where we want to discuss the results with them, face validity is a useful test attribute. If a client receives an absurd-looking test, he or she is highly likely to regard the whole business as pointless. Heim (1975) has made this point concerning the test items in interest tests which force subjects to choose between two equally loathsome occupations, for example (a) would you prefer to see round a bank, or (b) a sewage works?

For vocational guidance it is clear that the most important aspects of validity are predictive and construct validity. Thus the information that is most relevant would be evidence that the test could predict success (or failure) at certain occupations. If a test is capable of such predictive discrimination, it is not only a fine test, but one ideal for guidance, for this is precisely what we ultimately hope to achieve with our tests. Even concurrent correlations with occupational success would be useful.

The second line of evidence concerning the validity of tests for vocational guidance falls under the heading of construct validity. The best evidence of test ability would be an ability to discriminate between occupational groups. Again such a capacity is close to what we are trying to do in the course of vocational guidance. Thus predictive and discriminant validity of this kind are ideal for tests to be used in vocational guidance.

For vocational guidance it is a great advantage to have norms for as many different occupational groups as possible. For this we need sufficiently large and representative samples. Certainly for large and populous professions such as accountancy or law, samples of less than 100 would have to be treated with considerable caution. Smaller numbers could be tolerated for occupational groups that consist of few practitioners.

Certainly a test that was reliable, discriminating, showed good correlations with occupational success, differences among occupational groups and had good norms would be ideal for vocational guidance. One point needs to be stressed here. It is unlikely that a test measuring a single variable could discriminate between *many* occupational groups or have good correlations with success in a variety of jobs with the exception, of course, of intelligence, which as Ghiselli (1966) has shown is remarkably able to correlate with success in almost any job. However, one variable should be able to correlate with success in one or two occupations and to make a few discriminations among occupational groups. Multi-variable tests such as Cattell's *Sixteen Personality Factor Test (16PF)* (Cattell et al., 1970) can make many such discriminations.

OTHER QUALITIES USEFUL FOR VOCATIONAL GUIDANCE

In vocational guidance, as in most other branches of applied psychology, there is necessarily a limited amount of time for seeing clients. Since in vocational guidance, in the present state of the art in testing, test scores need to be supplemented by sensitive interviewing, testing time is even more at a premium. For this reason tests should be as short as is consonant with reliability. Brief tests allow, obviously, more tests to be given and thus more information can be acquired about the client. Thus brevity is an advantage for tests that are to be used in vocational guidance.

Since discussion is important and useful it is often sensible to choose tests in which the actual items can form a basis for such discussion. Thus, if in an extraversion test, for example, our subject has claimed that he does not like lively parties we can use this response as a basis for further probing. 'I see you say you don't like parties. What don't you like about them...?' In this way tests have a dual purpose of stimulating discussion and of yielding objective scores.

Psychological tests fall into two groups depending upon whether they have to be given on an individual basis or whether they may be administered to groups. For vocational guidance individual tests are excellent and these, of course, easily give rise to the discussions of subjects' answers that can be useful in this context. In general, therefore, there is no reason to avoid individual tests in vocational guidance.

The great advantage of group tests is that large numbers can be tested simultaneously. This can be useful in vocational guidance since it then gives the tester who may have only one session alone with any individual the time to discuss the subject's scores. Thus in vocational guidance whether group or individual tests are to be preferred depends upon the way the job is organized. Ideally it is better to see each person on his or her own on every occasion and thus individual tests are recommended (all other things being equal). However, where this is not possible, mass group testing followed up by individual discussion of the scores is a reasonable procedure.

CHARACTERISTICS OF TESTS REQUIRED FOR SELECTION

The demands of selection and vocational guidance are sufficiently distinct to make our choice of tests somewhat different, although always reliable, valid and well-standardized measures are essential.

A major difference concerns the motivation of subjects. In vocational guidance subjects are being helped. They, therefore, have little reason to try to deceive the psychologist, beyond the normal human response of wishing to be well thought of and attempting to hide imagined or real defects. In selection, however, this is not the case. Subjects wish to appear as brilliant as possible and to be suited to the job. What applicant for a sales position would admit, in a personality questionnaire, that he was unsociable, disliked or feared meeting people, thought commerce disagreeable and so on? This means that in selection, especially in the fields of personality, motivation and interests, tests with very obvious items should be avoided. Tests are best whose items are such that subjects are unsure what answer is best. In brief, face valid tests are not always ideal in selection because of the ease of faking.

In selection it is vital that tests be as reliable as possible, since, usually, decisions are made largely on the basis of test scores. Thus the standard error of score must be as low as possible. This is not only a question of psychometric efficiency but also one of ethics. For a psychologist to participate in a procedure that may radically affect individuals' careers and lives when he or she knows that those procedures are riddled with error is a serious matter.

Similarly validity is absolutely essential for selection tests. Hence the type of validity which is most valuable is that which is directly relevant to the process of selection. Ideally if we were to select for jobs X and Y we should demand evidence that our tests can discriminate between people in those jobs and controls, or that the scores correlate, either concurrently or predictively, with success at X or Y. Another approach to the question of validity for selection tests can be more general. If we have good evidence or are a priori convinced that variable X is implicated in job success or satisfaction, then the validity of that test is relevant. Here construct validity is all important.

In all these instances norms are clearly of vital importance, because essentially we are looking for high scorers on the test variable and we can only feel certain that scores are high if we can be confident that the normative data in the test manual is reliable. Thus good norms on relevant groups are essential. For this the ideal norms are for large and representative samples of the relevant occupational groups.

What other characteristics of psychological tests are required for selection depends much upon the way the selection procedure is organized. If, for example, as in the Armed Forces, large numbers of subjects have to be tested, group tests are essential. Individual tests can be used only where we are testing a very small number of candidates and have been allocated several hours with each individual. This, in practice, is a rare event. Short but reliable tests are the most practical.

There is one other point that needs discussion in selecting the best tests. So far I have assumed that we know what variables are related to occupational success – a knowledge which certainly makes our choice of test easier. Often, however, this is by no means the case. Here we have to use our common sense. This means that we would like to get measures of as wide a variety of variables as possible. This, again, forces us to choose brief tests. Indeed, it is a general rule in applied psychology that, given a test is reliable, the shorter the better. This is especially true for selection, where our knowledge of the critical variables is uncertain. The more information that can be used the more likely it is that we can arrive at a sensible decision. However, this does not mean that apparently totally irrelevant variables be measured. Common sense and general professional knowledge should be used to cut these out.

Tests for Special Groups

If we are needing to test special groups for example, handicapped children, brain damaged adults, the psychiatrically ill, special care has to be taken over the selection of tests. The reason for this is that among special groups the reliability and validity of a test may be radically changed. Some examples will clarify this point. In testing immigrant children who know little English, the *Raven's Matrices* (Raven, 1965) which is certainly a good non-verbal test of intelligence might be thought ideal. Nevertheless, cross-cultural studies (for example, Vernon, 1969) demonstrate that its factor-loadings vary in different groups. This certainly means its validity must be changing. Similarly among people with schizophrenia I would have no confidence, on general psychological arguments concerning loss of contact with reality, that a test designed for the normal population would remain valid. This means that when using a test for special groups it is essential that the test you choose has been shown to be reliable and valid within those groups. If it has not then a pilot study is required to show that it will work efficiently before the test is used for any substantive purpose.

This, of course, raises the question of how different from the normative groups must a group be before it demands further data collection. Any group that is likely to respond differently from normals on a test on account of language problems, cultural differences, psychological disturbance or age, falls into this category. Where such special groups are tested, tests should be chosen, which have been shown to work among such groups, as mentioned above. If no such tests exist pilot studies are necessary.

Discussion of the problems of selecting the best tests for special groups leads naturally to the difficulties involved in selecting the tests most suitable for children. Here, however, although there are considerable problems the rules are relatively simple. It is essential that the tests that are chosen are reliable and valid for the ages of children in the sample. It is quite wrong to think that a test that works well with 11-year-olds will be good for seven-year-olds or 15-year-olds. In ability tests the items are likely to be at the wrong level of difficulty and in the case of personality and motivation tests the items will not be relevant. 'Do you enjoy parties?' has quite different implications for adolescents than for seven-year-olds.

For tests of ability except where they are very long and have items for a wide span of age groups, subjects to be tested should not vary by more than about a year from those in the test handbook. Ideally subjects should be the age of those for whom the test was designed. For tests of personality and motivation, 3-year age bands are possible. Thus, 7–11, 12–15 and 16+ are quite common categories for children and adult personality tests. In brief, when testing children, ensure that the chosen test has been shown to be valid and reliable with the children of the age in the group you wish to test. There should also be norms for this age group.

Many of the best known and most carefully constructed psychological tests were developed in America. Hence their norms, however extensive, are not appropriate for use in Great Britain. In general, therefore, it is unwise to use an American test unless it has been standardized in Great Britain. Without these, British norms comparisons can be highly misleading.

SUMMARY

In this discussion on selecting the best test for vocational guidance, selection and for use in special groups, the essential elements are clear: our test should be shown to be reliable in the group we are testing and valid in such groups for the purposes for which we intend to use it.

From all the discussion so far there is one core issue that bears upon the suitability of tests and this concerns the relation of the normative groups to the subjects that we wish to test. Given that a test is valid and reliable, all turns upon whether the norms are suited for our subjects. Thus to conclude this chapter, I shall discuss the interpretation of scores on tests relative to normative groups and the problems of defining special groups at all.

Normative Groups

In the development of test norms sampling the normative groups is a major difficulty. The problem is most simple, in principle, in the setting up of age groups for there can be no doubt whether a child is 15 or not, for example. In the establishment of age norms, therefore, the only difficulty lies in ensuring that our sample of the age group is representative, in terms of social status, education and urban rural location, to name but three important demographic variables. Nevertheless since the methods of random and stratified sampling are well known, this problem is essentially practical – having sufficient funds and time to test sufficient subjects.

However, the sampling of other groups is by no means so simple. In this chapter I have written somewhat simplistically of accountants and other occupational groups. However, accountants are probably not homogeneous. Accountants in private practice are probably different from those working for the large accountancy firms and these probably differ again from the accountants employed by companies, and who often dominate company policy. In setting up normative accountant groups, therefore, all these should be sampled, and if there are differences, a separate group of each type would be best.

If accountants differ, they probably do so less than do teachers. Primary, secondary and further education teachers certainly require separate norms and probably it is best if teachers are further split into subject groups. Without denigrating any groups, I am confident that mathematics, domestic science and drama teachers are very different in more than just abilities as indeed evidence from the 16PF *Manual* (Cattell et al., 1970) suggests. This certainly implies that as a normative group 'teachers' will not do.

When we come to the formation of pathological or abnormal groups, the problems become complex. First of all there is little agreement among psychiatrists when classifying subjects. This is the problem that has bedeviled the *Minnesota Multiphasic Personality Inventory (MMPI*, Hathaway and McKinley, 1951) where items were chosen because they discriminated between one psychiatric group and another. Even if there is good agreement many psychologists and psychiatrists use categories which are so different that the sets are mutually incompatible. Terms such as 'neurotic', 'psychotic' and 'schizophrenic' are far too vague and complex to be used as the basis for norms.

This difficulty in the meaning of criterion, normative groups, other than age groups, means that the interpretation of an individual's score relative to norms must be extremely cautious. This is particularly so because norms, even where the means are significantly different, usually overlap to a considerable extent. In interpreting an individual's score all we must say is that the score resembles that of a particular group. The meaning of this must be interpreted taking all that subject's other scores into account as well as biographical information. The routine 'blind' use of scores and norms is likely to be highly misleading.

I shall give a few examples from the *Handbook* to the *Sixteen Personality Factor Test* (16PF) where an heroic attempt has been made to provide useful norms. Scientists generally are low on Factor A (warmth vs aloofness). The norms here consist of 96 biologists, 161 chemists and chemical engineers, 21 geologists (Australian), 91 physicists and 107 psychologists. All were male. Even one glance reveals considerable problems: no female norms; all these scientists (other than the Australians) were American; very small numbers if a representative sample is required; no information is given about the provenance of these samples. Interpretations must be cautious, therefore. However, if we consider Factor A, suppose that our subject obtained a score of 4. This would put him close to the scientist's mean. We could argue that he resembled the scientists in the normative sample, but while this is true it is also the case that British artists have a mean of 4! However, here the N is only 27 so extreme caution has to be shown. Our subject on Factor A resembles both artists and scientists.

All this difficulty in interpretation can be resolved if we know what are the salient features of any group. Then if our subject resembles the group on all these variables, perhaps some sense can be made of the scores. Even so it is essential that the normative groups are large and representative. The *Cattell Norms*, although numerous, do sometimes fall short of these ideals: 1280 female elementary teachers – this is certainly a large sample; 88 male equivalents, a figure which is far too small; 89 writers; 81 university professors; 36 employment counsellors; 57 male swimmers; 41 Olympic champion athletes. With such samples, again, interpretation must be cautious.

In summary all that can be said about a subject's scores relative to norms is that he or she resembles or differs from certain groups. With a large number of variables some sense may be made of the set of scores. However, much depends upon the reliability and representativeness of the norms. Certainly without norms scores are meaningless. With norms due to the problems of establishing meaningful groups, interpretations can be made but great caution and common sense must be shown.

Conclusions

Our conclusions to this chapter can be simple and brief. For all purposes tests should be reliable, valid, discriminating and have good norms. High reliability is essential to minimize the standard error of score. Validity is a more subjective index and validity is always to be measured with reference to a particular purpose. This is important in selecting our tests for a normally valid test may not be so as we wish to use it. The particular validity of a test must be taken into account, therefore, in the different contexts of guidance and selection and it is particularly important where special groups are tested. Norms are essential for test interpretation. However, while this is so there are considerable problems in the establishment of norms, both practical and conceptual problems concerned with the homogeneity of groups and the reliability of normative categories. In the light of this, comparison of individuals' scores with norms must be very cautious and far from automatic.

References

BUROS, O.K. (1978). *The VIII Mental Measurement Year Book*. Highland Park, N.J.: Gryphon Press.

CATTELL, R.B., EBER, H.W. & TATSUOKA, M.M. (1970). *The 16PF Test*. Champaign, Illinois: IPAT.

FERGUSON, G.A. (1949). On the theory of test development. *Psychometrika, 14*, 61–8.

GHISELLI, E.E. (1966). *The Validity of Occupational Aptitude Tests*. New York: Wiley.

HATHAWAY, S.R. & MCKINLEY, J.C. (1951). *The Minnesota Multiphasic Personality Inventory*. New York: Psychological Corporation.

HEIM, A. (1975). *Psychological Testing*. London: Oxford University Press.

HOYT, C. (1941). Test reliability obtained by analysis of variance. *Psychometrika, 6*, 153–60.

KLINE, P. (1975). *The Psychology of Vocational Guidance*. London: Batsford.

LORD, F.M. (1974). *Individualised Testing and Item Characteristic Cume Theory*. Princeton: E.T.S.

RAVEN, J.C. (1965). *Progressive Matrices*. London: H.K. Lewis.

VERNON, P.E. (1950). *The Measurement of Abilities*. London: University of London Press.

VERNON, P.E. (1969). *Intelligence and Cultural Environment*. London: Methuen.

Assessing the Individual: Examples within the Clinical Setting

6

Tim Pring

The most casual student of psychometrics will be familiar with the need to standardize tests and to assess their reliability and validity. Standardization, in particular, is central to any effort that attempts to assess individual behaviours against a broader background. For instance, by converting test scores to z-scores (see page 22) an individual's behaviour may be compared with the general population norms supplied with the test. Additionally, performance on more than one standardized test allows us to assess differences in performance across tasks within the same individual.

These points are well known. Consequently, it may be somewhat surprising that much useful information can be acquired by testing with more informal tests that often fail to fulfil these requirements. This chapter examines two areas of clinical intervention. Despite contrasting theoretical positions each has found it necessary to make use of in-depth studies of single or small numbers of patients whose behaviour and response to treatment can often only be measured in this way. The first is the use of the techniques of behaviourist psychology to modify behaviours that may be either distressing to the client or socially unacceptable to others. Such behaviour modification approaches are widely used in clinical psychology and a variety of clinical settings, and the need to demonstrate the efficacy of the treatment interventions employed has led to the development of a range of single subject experimental designs by which clinical interventions may be assessed. The second area concerns the cognitive impairments that may follow damage to the brain. Traditionally such study is the province of the neuropsychologist. Currently, however, a productive exchange of ideas between neuropsychology and cognitive psychology has been taking place. The resulting discipline, cognitive neuropsychology, has placed great emphasis on detailed assessment of individual patients for which only informal testing procedures may be available. Subsequently, the need to evaluate the treatments used may call for the application of single subject experimental designs similar to those employed in behaviour modification.

There are a variety of reasons why such informal assessment procedures may be necessary. One factor is that the need to compare performance with that of the population may be much reduced because the behaviours to be assessed and treated may be abnormal by almost any criterion; the need is rather to understand their causes and assess their response to treatment. A second is that the behaviours to be assessed may be extremely idiosyncratic. In the case of behaviour modification techniques, the behaviours treated may be both highly individual and situation specific. Formal assessments are unlikely to capture such individuality; assessments that are specific to individuals and specific behaviours and which may be used in real situations are more appropriate. A similar situation has now arisen within neuropsychology. Traditionally this has proceeded by using large-scale batteries of tests and identifying groups of patients who share similar patterns of deficits. Typically these patients might be expected to share similar sites of brain damage so that correspondences might be built up between clusters of behavioural impairments and brain anatomy. Such an approach is founded on the reasonable assumption that patients can be found with substantial similarities of behavioural deficits. Consequently, it looks for behaviours that associate with one another and, in turn, may be associated with different areas of damage within the brain. Such an approach implicitly suggests that the individual may be compared with a peer group. By contrast the cognitive neuropsychological approach has looked for dissociations of functions both within a patient's functioning and between patients, arguing that these are more informative about the detailed breakdown of processing stages. Thus testing is likely to be both more detailed and more individually orientated.

An Experimental Basis for Individual Assessment

Despite these qualifications, the seemingly open invitation to create and apply unstandardized tests to individuals may appear a very undisciplined procedure. An element of discipline is introduced by the essentially experimental nature of the investigations pursued, however. Thus, in studies of the effects of behavioural therapy, care has been taken to develop and employ single-case experimental designs (described below) in which periods of treatment and no treatment are compared. Changes in behaviour can then be demonstrated to occur both when treatment is introduced and when it is withdrawn. Although questions may still be asked about the long-term effects of such interventions and about their ability to generalize to nonclinical situations, it would appear undeniable that a link between the treatment and its immediate behavioural consequences has been shown.

A similar situation exists in the investigation of cognitive impairments suffered after brain damage and may be demonstrated by a simple example. Suppose a patient's reading ability has been damaged so that he or she is forced to read by converting print directly to phonology. In many languages, including English, the occurrence of irregular spellings will be a problem to such a patient. The presence of such a problem may be readily assessed by comparing the patient's reading of regular and irregular words. All that is required are sets of such words which have been matched on other variables such as frequency and length (which might influence performance for other reasons). If an effect of regularity still emerges it may be assumed that the patient is at least partially dependent on a phonological strategy for reading and that alternative reading abilities have been damaged. This is because irregular words (such as *yacht*) generate erroneous phonological codes if a phonological strategy is used. This assessment becomes, in effect, a small experiment in which other variables have been controlled. The subject's overall performance and its relation to that of other patients and to normal readers is less important than the demonstration of a selectively greater deficit for irregular than regular words (the significance of which can be assessed by a Chi Square test). Such a finding directly informs us about (one of) the patient's problems. Furthermore such findings may invite specialized forms of treatment that may also be assessed using single subject experimental designs.

Compared with the statistically based techniques outlined in this book, this single case design approach might seem to be lacking in stringency. For the experienced psychometric test user, it might seem almost casual. Foremost among the precautions offered to users of these designs is the inability to generalize results to other subjects. Since a single subject can in no sense represent a random sample of any population, no population exists to which results may be generalized. As previously emphasized, however, generalization may be inappropriate since use of the approach implicitly recognizes the individuality of the subject tested. Alternatively the generality of findings must be sought by replication. In many other respects, however, these designs contain recognizable elements of true experiments. It is possible to state an hypothesis, to recognize dependent and independent variables and controls are available to eliminate the influences of extraneous variables. Equally it is important that the behaviours being observed are clearly defined and that their reliability both across observations within the same observer and between observers is established.

The Single Subject Approach in a Clinical Setting

The single subject approach to research is one that presents several advantages to those working in a clinical setting. The heterogeneity of patients' problems has already been mentioned. This not only makes it difficult to assemble groups of similar subjects, but threatens the ability of traditional group research designs to obtain useful information. If subjects are not sufficiently similar it will be difficult to justify presenting the same treatment to them, alternatively if differing treatments are offered it will be difficult to assess their individual effects regardless of the overall result in terms of statistical significance. Moreover, variability of response to treatment may be the rule rather than the exception when dealing with clinical groups. Such variability can only be increased if the definition of the target group is uncertain and if differing treatments are offered to different patients. Under such circumstances it is difficult for group designs to obtain significant results and it is easy to conclude that treatment does not work despite the possibility that individual patients may have made substantial progress. In addition clinical practice clearly offers severe practical difficulties to the conduct of orthodox group studies by those whose primary duty is to offer treatment rather than to carry out research.

Peck (1985) has pointed out that the assumption is too readily made that use of single case studies in clinical psychology is limited to treatments involving behaviour modification. The latter part of this chapter describes their use in a quite different setting. Despite this it is undeniably the case that they are well suited to and have been extensively developed within the behaviourist approach to treatment. Within this approach two distinct stages can be identified. In the first the nature of the client's problems must be identified and hypotheses formed about the causes of behaviours and the means of altering them. The second consists of choosing an appropriate experimental design and assessing the consequences of the treatment used.

IDENTIFYING THE PROBLEM

The behaviourist approach suggests that behaviours have their antecedents in reinforcing aspects of the subject's environment. A major step in understanding either behaviours which are present but unwanted or more desirable behaviours which have failed to develop is to observe the environmental events which either reinforce or fail to reinforce these behaviours. This functional analysis of behaviour should have as its goal an hypothesis about the causes of behaviours and the possible means of changing them which can then be tested by demonstrating a successful treatment intervention.

A good description of the problems involved in this process has been provided by Yule (1980). Clearly a general difficulty is that there will rarely be objective means available for measuring behaviours. Observational techniques will normally be necessary both at the stage at which hypotheses are being formed and at the stage at which they are being tested. It is important that target behaviours should be closely defined, therefore, and inter-tester reliability may provide an important indication that this has been achieved.

SINGLE SUBJECT EXPERIMENTAL DESIGNS

Single subject experimental designs are now in extensive use for assessing the effects of treatment interventions. These designs, sometimes referred to as time series designs, monitor behaviour over periods in which treatment is not applied (the A phase) and then when it is applied (the B phase). The designs have been widely described (see for example Barlow and Hersen, 1985, Kazdin, 1982 and Peck, 1985) so that a detailed description is unnecessary here.

Some examples of the designs are shown in Box 6.1. The simplest available design is an AB design in which the initial period acts as a baseline for changes in behaviour which might be occurring independently of treatment and the second period monitors the effect of implementing treatment. Many authors (for example, Kazdin, 1982) express dissatisfaction with this design that only allows for one transition between no treatment and treatment. Consequently, the ABA design, Box 6.1a, which allows for a return to no treatment and thus allows for a correspondence between intervention and its consequences to be twice observed becomes the simplest acceptable design. Once the principle of multiphase designs is accepted there is little limit to the range of designs that may be used. Treatment may be successively applied and removed (for instance, ABAB), alternative treatments may be compared (ABACA), and so on, where C is a second form of treatment, Box 6.1b, or the combined effects of treatments may be compared with their individual effects (ABACA(BC)A). A conflict in the use of these designs may immediately be identified. A requirement of the methodology

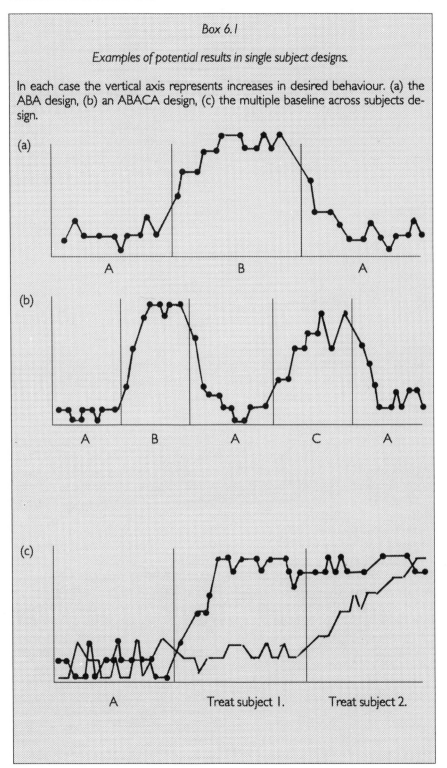

Box 6.1

Examples of potential results in single subject designs.

In each case the vertical axis represents increases in desired behaviour. (a) the ABA design, (b) an ABACA design, (c) the multiple baseline across subjects design.

is that later periods of no treatment should show a decline in the previous gains through treatment. This requirement contradicts the clinician's hopes that successful therapy will both generalize beyond the clinic and be maintained once an inevitable decision has been made to cease treatment.

Further alternatives are offered by multiple baseline designs. In these multiple transitions between no treatment and treatment are achieved by applying it to different but similar subjects at different times (multiple baselines across subjects, Box 6.1(c)), to the same behaviour in the same subject but in different situations at different times (multiple baselines across situations) or to different behaviours at different times in the same subject (multiple baselines across behaviour).

In practice designs are often used which are individually suited to the requirements of the treatment situation and which combine elements of the designs above. An example will illustrate this. Odom et al. (1985) conducted an investigation to demonstrate that social interaction could be increased between preschool children and their handicapped peers. Three handicapped children were involved (so that the design was a multiple baseline across subjects). After establishing a baseline, treatment consisted of prompts from teachers to initiate interaction and direct reinforcement in the form of tokens. Interactions increased but did not generalize to other situations. However, use of a multiple baseline across situations did demonstrate that extending the treatment to other situations was effective. The initial AB design was then extended by removing the token reinforcement. This did not substantially affect the number of interactions but a further stage in which teacher prompts were also removed did. In a final phase prompts were reintroduced and interactions again increased. In sum the combination of different design features presents a convincing picture that the use of prompting can increase interactions although it appears unlikely that the effects generalize outside the immediate treatment context. Obviously the experiment included a number of events such as prompts and interactions whose occurrence must be observationally assessed. Interobserver reliability coefficients are accordingly calculated for those demonstrating that their operational definitions were sufficiently clear to allow close agreement between observers.

These designs are ideally suited to the application of behavioural interventions but (as we shall see) present some difficulties when transferred to other situations. One advantage is the relative lack of specificity between the form of the intervention and the behaviour to be treated. Treatments will usually take the form of substituting one form of reinforcement for another which, it is hypothesized, has given rise to the abnormal behaviour. The same treatment may be equally successful in dealing with quite different forms of behaviour (as is illustrated in the multiple baseline across behaviours design). Furthermore, the effects of these treatments are often rapid and easily detected, and when removed result in detectable deteriorations in behaviour. As a consequence use of designs in which treatment is both implemented and removed is feasible and, though there has been some debate on the issue of statistical analysis, many practitioners feel that the rapid and substantial shifts in behaviour that are often observed are sufficiently convincing without formal statistical analysis. Moreover, it is often argued that substantial shifts in behaviour are necessary to present convincing evidence of clinical improvement as opposed to merely statistically detectable changes.

Single Case Studies in Neuropsychology

Testing procedures in cognitive neuropsychology may be divided into two distinct sections. The first consists of tests used to investigate the deficits experienced by patients. This chapter will limit itself to examples of deficits in language abilities. As previously stressed the emphasis has been on the individuality of patients' problems. Consequently the range of tests that might be used is unlimited. A further point is that many of these tests have been created in the cause of theoretical investigations of patients rather than directly for clinical use. Some of these tests have become quite widely used in clinical work although most remain unstandardized. These procedures have sometimes been called 'alternative tests' to distinguish them from the longer standing test batteries which assess skills across a broader range and which are often standardized on appropriate patient populations.

The second section concerns the assessment of treatment and is more directly the concern of the clinician. The designs described above have been influential here although circumstances will require some modification.

ASSESSING THE PATIENT'S PROBLEMS

Figure 6.1 depicts a simplified form of a model developed to explain single word processing. It depicts the stages by which spoken or written single words and pictures may be understood and repeated, read or named aloud. In the case of all three modalities of input depicted in the figure — that is, pictures, spoken and written words — there is an initial perceptual analysis, not shown in the figure. It is generally agreed that this involves the processing of features and their interconnections. This information can then transfer to the semantic system, word phonology and to the response buffer via the routes indicated in the figure. The figure illustrates that from the perceptual level there can be access to the semantic system (for instance, recognizing that a picture represents a dog at the conceptual level), then the word phonology is retrieved (in this case the word unit representing 'dog'). This entails accessing the required sequence of phonemes (/d/, /o/ and /g/) from the auditory lexicon. The response buffer, which does not have direct access to the auditory lexicon, provides the means for articulating these assembled phonemes and the final part is the actual articulation or speech.

The version presented is both a simplified one (see Ellis, 1982 and Morton, 1985) and one that avoids several current disputes (see Humphreys and Evett, 1985 and Shallice, 1987). Nevertheless, there is substantial evidence for and agreement about the broad form of the model.

Its chief value in clinical work is as a conceptual aid to testing and assessing the problems patients experience at this level. Armed with such a framework patients' problems may be assessed with the informal sorts of tests described above. The tests should be experimental, however, in the sense that they test hypotheses about the patients' difficulties and use

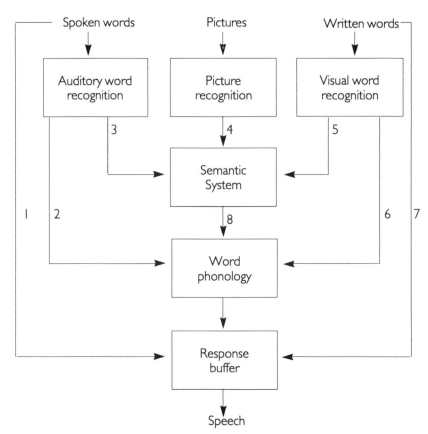

Figure 6.1: Simplified model of the procedures involved in processing single spoken or written words and pictures

stimuli which are controlled on some dimensions while testing the effects of others.

Some relatively simple examples will assist here. Consider a patient who had damage to pathway 3. Such a patient would present with a serious problem in auditory comprehension. If tested with any task that required access to semantics from auditory input (for instance, classifying or categorizing stimuli, matching pairs of stimuli for similarity of meaning, matching spoken stimuli to pictures or written words) the patient will fail. Nevertheless he or she would be able to repeat spoken stimuli either by route 2 which can access the phonology of known words or by route 1 which can convert any auditory verbal stimuli (whether or not a known word) to phonology. Equally he would be able to distinguish between known words and novel verbal stimuli by accessing the auditory word recognition system. With such a patient we might wonder whether the deficit was limited to auditory input; that is, does the problem disconnect auditory input from intact semantic ability or is semantic ability itself impaired? This may readily be assessed by applying similar semantic tests (to those used auditorily) in the pictorial or written modalities. A patient who fared poorly in all three might reasonably be expected to have a general deficit in his or her semantic ability.

Now suppose that the same patient has further damage to pathway 8. Such a patient will experience difficulty in naming pictures presented though he or she should be able to adequately understand them. Typically such patients will have similar word-finding problems in spontaneous speech. In the present case, however, the patient should be able to both understand (by route 5) and read aloud (by route 6) written words so that a difference should be apparent between naming of pictures and the reading aloud of the words they represent.

Finally, let us suppose that route 6 is also damaged. The patient will now comprehend written words adequately but his or her reading aloud of them will be subject to the same problem encountered in naming pictures with one exception. This is that route 7 remains operative. This route is capable of converting printed words directly into their phonological form so that they may be read aloud. As in the example at the beginning of this chapter use of such a route can be detected by finding a difference in the reading of regular and irregular words which have been matched on other variables such as frequency and length. In the present case all such words might be understood adequately, but in the presence of the deficits in routes 6 and 8 reading aloud would occur by route 7 giving the advantage for regular words.

The description so far has been simplified in at least two ways. First, it is rarely the case that patients are found who have such specific damage that a single route is damaged in isolation from some damage to other stages in the processing model. Second, the hypothetical patient described above has been presented as if the nature of the damage was total. In fact damage is much more likely to show partial effects upon processing and these may in turn be detectable by showing that success in processing particular words is a function of such variables as word frequency or length. The hypothesized damage to route 8 above provides a good example. Such damage would be most obviously expressed in word finding problems. This would be apparent in spontaneous speech but more directly testable by asking the patient to name pictures. Typically this task may be met with partial success but also with failure to name many obviously clear and familiar pictures. However, failures to name may be of various kinds. Patients may merely fail or may give circumlocutionary responses. The latter serve to illustrate that the patient has obtained a fairly adequate semantic knowledge of the stimuli but cannot access its phonology. Alternatively, errors may take the form of phonological distortions which are, nevertheless, recognizably the correct name or may be semantically related but otherwise dissimilar items. In the former case it is tempting to believe that the correct phonology is being accessed but that some problem arises in realizing this in speech. In the latter case it may be assumed that the origins of the patient's problems lie in identifying the precise semantic specification of the picture. Such an interpretation is supported by the fact that such patients also show similar semantic confusion in tasks which only require comprehension and not a spoken response. This last example again illustrates a case in which the effects of damage upon our model is not all-or-none but rather a subtle distortion of normal processing.

Patients such as in the above example are described as anomic. Frequently their naming can be aided by providing a phonological cue such as the first sound of the word or by giving a contextual or other form of semantic cue. Although there remain gaps in our understanding of the causes of the different forms of responses they may make and their relationship to the assistance that may be obtained from various forms of cues, it is clear that informal tests administered to an individual patient may give much information about the types of error made. Such tests might, for example, examine the effects of phonological complexity, length and frequency on naming. The occurrence of semantic problems may also be tested. Typically patients who make semantic errors in naming will show semantic deficits in other tasks. They may also show a selective deficit for abstract concepts as against concrete concepts which may be assessed by testing such items matched for other relevant variables such as frequency and length.

This fairly lengthy digression into cognitive neuropsychology hopefully illustrates points previously made. First, that testing of individual patients with informal tests of this kind can be clinically informative even though the tests are unstandardized. Second, that such testing may be disciplined by an experimental approach in which the effects of certain variables are controlled while those of others are assessed. The objective of such testing is to improve understanding and, consequently, improve treatment of the patient's problems. It is unfortunately the case that, at present, too little is known about the effects of treatment and the appropriateness of different forms of treatment for different patients. Expanding knowledge on this issue is therefore an important priority. The best that can be said at present is that choice of treatment is likely to be better informed the more specifically we understand the patient's difficulties and that the effects of treatment for more specifically defined problems may be more readily detected.

ASSESSING THE EFFECTS OF TREATMENT

There are several problems that will need to be overcome if beneficial effects of treatment for language deficits of the kind above are to be demonstrated. First, such patients undergo a period of spontaneous recovery in the first months after brain insult from which the effects of treatment will need to be dissociated. An obvious possibility is to treat the patient at a period after such recovery but this alternative is frequently neither practical nor ethical. Second, any assessments of the effects of treatment need to discover whether the effects are due to the specific treatment offered or whether they are general effects of receiving any form of clinical attention. Third, there is the issue of whether the effects of treatment generalize beyond the specific items used in therapy. As will be seen below this consideration will have an important bearing on the choice of an experimental design for assessing the treatment. Finally, there is the issue of generalization of the benefits of therapy beyond the clinical situation. Any form of assessment of treatment is likely to face difficulties with this issue and the designs below do not directly address it.

DESIGNS USING OTHER ITEMS AS CONTROLS

A wide variety of designs might be used to assess therapy each affording varying degrees of success with the above problems. The simplest design assumes that the effects of treatment are limited to the immediate items treated. In this case a matched set of items on which the patient performs equally poorly prior to treatment may be used as a control. Such a situation can be illustrated by a study of therapy for anomia conducted on a patient R.S. by Marshall (unpublished).

R.S. presented with a fairly severe word finding problem. When naming pictures he appeared to have adequate semantic knowledge of the concept involved but difficulty in finding its phonological form. This analysis was confirmed by the fact that he never made semantic misnamings in his responses and on a selection of tasks testing the semantic system he performed well in all modalities of presentation. Additionally he was able to read aloud many words whose pictures he could not name.

From this performance it was assumed that R.S.'s major problem lay in route 8 (Figure 6.1). Previous studies of groups of patients (Howard et al., 1985) have suggested that use of tasks requiring semantic decisions to stimulus items but not requiring their overt naming benefits subsequent naming of the items. Despite the fact that R.S. showed no apparent difficulty in such tasks it was decided to test their effects on his naming. Two groups of pictures were assembled such that naming success with each was equally poor prior to treatment. One group was then treated, the others acting as controls. A typical task used in treatment consisted of matching pictures from the treated group against one of a series of semantically related written items. This utilized two tasks which were within the patient's capabilities. A semantic decision had to be made; additionally phonology of the picture names could be accessed via R.S.'s ability to read aloud. After such treatment R.S. was significantly more likely to name pictures in the experimental set than in the untreated controls (since the pre-treatment performance on the two sets was equal, the post-treatment scores could be directly compared using a Chi Square test).

The improvement shown here suggests that use of semantic tasks can benefit subsequent word finding performance even when they do not, themselves, require naming. Other studies have confirmed this and shown that it may also benefit patients who are much less proficient at the semantic decisions required and at reading aloud than was R.S. This form of approach can only be used when the effects of treatment do not generalize to untreated items. In the domain of language tasks this may be exceptional and it may also be thought that the gains from treatment are somewhat limited as a result. Despite this the approach is a straightforward one and may be readily extended preferably, in the first instance, by treating and demonstrating improvement in the control set of pictures. Moreover the view that there is no generalization at all is probably incorrect. R.S., when tested on pictures of items used as semantically related foils in the treatment above, was able to name at above 90 per cent accuracy. Generalization appears to be occurring within the semantic areas represented by these pictures.

USING ANOTHER TASK AS A CONTROL

More frequently the major objective of treatment may be to reinstate a particular language skill. Suppose, for example, a patient demonstrates an auditory comprehension deficit at the sentence level. Such patients may adequately comprehend the constituent words of the sentence but be unable to construct a meaning based upon the syntactic structures used. Attempts to restore this ability, however, would be expected to improve comprehension of a wide variety of sentences so that the approach used above would be inappropriate.

How then can we demonstrate successful treatment in this situation? A popular solution has been to treat one area of functioning while using an unrelated and untreated area as a control. If the control does not improve while the treated area does it can be argued that this improvement is due to treatment and not to naturally occurring recovery. But there are a number of reasons for feeling uneasy about this approach. What, for example, constitutes an unrelated task? In the example above ability to comprehend written sentences would clearly be inappropriate as it might reasonably be expected to improve with auditory comprehension. Suppose that a task such as ability to form grammatically well-formed sentences were used instead. Here the question of relatedness is less clear since opinion is still divided on whether syntactic abilities or disabilities act independently in comprehension and production or whether some form of parallelism exists. In view of this, selection of an unambiguously unrelated task is indicated. In the above example ability to spell correctly written words might constitute such a task. Tasks which more obviously qualify as unrelated carry their own problems however. At the theoretical level can we be sure that spontaneous recovery, if present, will equally affect two tasks that are cognitively less related? At the psychometric level can we be sure that our means of measuring more disparate tasks are equally sensitive to change in the two areas. Clearly choice of a suitable control task is problematical here; at the extreme it is possible to select a control which (unfairly) will be very unlikely to show improvement. The only obvious means of avoiding this dilemma is to incorporate a further stage into the design in which, following treatment of the first area, treatment is also offered for the control task. This would, of course, be another form of treatment and would demonstrate that the control task was itself open to successful treatment. In this design, therefore, the initial period represents a contrast between progress in a treated task and an untreated one and the second stage represents a demonstration that the control task may also improve with treatment. During this second stage the opportunity also occurs to monitor the first task after treatment has been withdrawn. This would bring the design close to the crossover treatment design (Coltheart, 1983) which is described below. This design now represents a more disciplined approach. It is, however, more difficult to implement in clinical situations and invites possible ambiguous results when one area of functioning appears to respond to a treatment but the other does not.

USING THE TREATED TASK AS ITS OWN CONTROL

As we have seen the two designs above may both have limited application. The first may only be used when the effects of treatment are expected to be limited to the immediate items used in treatment. In the rehabilitation of cognitive skills we shall often be concerned with reinstating a skill that may be expected to generalize to other items. The second design can deal with this problem but only at the expense of uncertainty about the appropriate control task. The most obvious solution, therefore, appears to be the adoption of the form of designs used in behaviour modification studies and already described above.

Although these designs can be used there are, as mentioned earlier, a number of new problems to be confronted that may make many of the more methodologically satisfactory designs unworkable. First among these is the assumption, usually fulfilled in behavioural treatments, that withdrawal of the treatment will cause a decline from previous progress. Where treatment aims to reinstate previously known skills and has been successful such a decline is unlikely. Indeed if a decline did occur we might doubt the efficacy of the treatment. Clearly there is a conflict here between the requirements of methodology and the realities of clinical work. The second problem also illustrates this. The designs previously described require that when two areas are treated, the same treatment (in the form of changes in reinforcement patterns) can be applied to each. This is again a methodological requirement since we need, for example when using multiple baseline designs, to demonstrate the effect of the treatment on more than one occasion. Clearly this requirement is unlikely to be met in cognitive rehabilitation where quite specific treatment approaches are likely to be required for different skills.

The implication of these problems appears to leave us only with the simple AB design which many practitioners are unwilling to accept as adequate. One response to this situation might be to contrast the more theoretical nature of many of the behavioural studies with the more immediate need for a means of assessing ongoing clinical interventions. In the latter, it might be argued, the demands of methodology are less important than the need to justify the treatment being adopted. An AB design can help to do the latter and the demands of methodology can be satisfied to some extent by replicating the approach when another similar patient becomes available (thus approximating to a multiple baseline across subjects design).

However, other difficulties may threaten our ability to use even the AB design. First, it might be objected that the need for periods of no treatment to obtain baselines is not acceptable. There appear to be two general solutions to this. In one, we could conduct our study against a background of more general ongoing therapy. Any effects that this has on progress in the experimental area would be present across both treatment and no treatment periods. Alternatively we could isolate two areas for study so that the patient was always receiving a specific therapy which was, in turn, being assessed. In practice this would probably mean combining an AB design with a BA design and would constitute what Coltheart (1983) calls the crossover treatment design. There are two problems. As with the discussion above there will be a need to choose two areas that are sufficiently unrelated to the extent that the treatment applied to one does not affect the other. Second, there is the possible ambiguity in the results that one treatment may show effects while the other does not. In particular the area treated during the first phase of the design might continue to improve in the second no-treatment phase as a result of the gains made in treatment. Such a result again threatens the requirements of the experimental methodology used.

Finally, there is again the problem of statistical analysis. Changes in experiments of this kind may be much smaller than in those using behavioural interventions so that some form of analysis is indicated. One approach may be merely to compare the number of items correctly answered on the assessment before and after treatment (using, for example, the McNemar test). Another alternative is to monitor progress throughout the different phases of the design by giving periodic assessments. Although this approach is rather time-consuming it does give continuous information about the patient's progress. A simple, though not very powerful, means of analysing this form of data is a nonparametric analysis of trend such as the Mann test (see Pring, 1986).

This general approach can again be illustrated by an example. A study by Merry (unpublished) was directed towards aiding retrieval of verbs in an agrammatic patient. Such patients produce speech which, though communicative in quality, may be both laboured in articulation and deficient in syntax. Typically, short grammatical words and affixes are omitted and the patient may have difficulty producing verbs. The patient (B.M.) in this study demonstrated a striking inability to retrieve verbs while being relatively proficient at retrieving related nouns. A form of therapy was devised in which B.M. was encouraged to use pictures of related noun objects to assist in the naming of verb pictures. Forty verbs were used which B.M. had failed to name at the beginning of the study. In half the stimuli the noun and verb names were both phonologically and semantically related, in the other half only a semantic relationship existed. By a series of steps B.M. developed a strategy in which he assisted the access of verb names by visualizing a related object.

The approach used here is to encourage the development of a strategy towards verb naming. If fully successful the patient should be able to apply it to other verbs not included in therapy. Consequently use of a design in which an untreated set of verbs was used as a control would be inappropriate. In this study the patient's progress was monitored over a 4-week period in which 8 assessments of the naming of 10 of the items drawn on each occasion at random from the 40 was made. Similar assessments were carried out during treatment. These assessments were subtracted so that the difference in the trends during baseline and treatment (Pring, 1986) could be assessed. This difference showed a significant effect of the treatment. At the end of treatment B.M. could name 33 of the verbs and 27 at a follow-up assessment six weeks later. Phonologically similar verbs fared somewhat, but not significantly, better than those with only a semantic relationship with the noun.

Conclusions

The above discussion has examined methods by which behaviours and changes in behaviours following treatments can be examined in two areas of clinical work. In contrast to most discussions of behavioural assessment issues relating to the standardization, reliability and validity of tests have been largely absent. Instead informal assessment procedures have been recommended that offer the advantage of giving specific information about the individual's behaviours. This testing has been disciplined to a degree by an experimental approach linked to an accumulation of theoretical ideas about the underlying causes of the behaviours treated.

The two areas discussed are in marked theoretical contrast. They also offer a clear contrast in their suitability for single case studies of their treatments. Behavioural treatments lend themselves to methodological rigour and to an extensive published literature. Cognitive remediation, in common with other areas of clinical work, presents a number of obstacles to such rigour. The methodologies available here are undoubtedly weak; nevertheless, they present the clinician with the opportunity to monitor treatment more clearly and to carry out, within clinical settings, experimental investigations of the effects of treatment.

References

BARLOW, D.H. & HERSEN, M. (1985). *Single Case Experimental Studies*. Oxford: Pergamon.

COLTHEART, M. (1983). Aphasia therapy research: a single case study approach. In C. CODE & D.J. MULLER (Eds), *Aphasia Therapy*. London: Arnold.

ELLIS, A.W. (1982). Spelling and writing (and reading and speaking). In A.W. ELLIS (Ed.) *Normality and Pathology in Cognitive Functions*. London: Academic Press.

HOWARD, D., PATTERSON, K., FRANKLIN, S., ORCHARD-LISLE, V. & MORTIN, J. (1985). Treatment of word retrieval deficits in aphasia. A comparison of two therapy methods. *Brain, 108,* 817–29.

HUMPHREYS, G.W. & EVETT, L. (1985). Are there independent lexical and non-lexical routes in reading? *The Behavioural and Brain Sciences, 8,* 689–740.

KAZDIN, A.E. (1982). *Single Case Designs: Methods for Clinical and Applied Settings*. New York: Oxford University Press.

MARSHALL, J. (unpublished). Unpublished study. Department of Clinical Communication Studies, The City University.

MORTON, J. (1985). Naming. In S. NEWMAN & R. EPSTEIN (Eds), *Current Perspectives in Dysphasia*. Edinburgh: Churchill Livingstone.

ODOM, S.L., HOWSON, M., JAMESON, B. & STRAIN, P.S. (1985). Increasing handicapped pre-schooler's peer social interactions: cross setting and component analysis. *Journal of Applied Behavior Analysis, 18,* 3–16.

PECK, D.F. (1985). Small N experimental designs in clinical research. In F.N. WATTS (Ed.), *New Developments in Clinical Psychology*. Chichester: Wiley.

PRING, T.R. (1986). Evaluating the effects of speech therapy for aphasics: developing the single case methodology. *British Journal of Disorders of Communication, 21,* 103–115.

SHALLICE, I. (1987). Impairments of semantic processing: Multiple dissociations. In M. COLTHEART, G. SARTORI & R. JOB (Eds), *The Cognitive Neuropsychology of Language*. London: Erlbaum.

YULE, W. (1980). Identifying problems – Functional analysis and observation and recording techniques. In W. YULE & J. CARR (Eds.), *Behaviour Modification for the Mentally Handicapped*. London: Croom Helm.

Computer-assisted Assessment

7

Chris French

For a testing system to be fully *automated* or *computerized* it would have to be able to perform all of the following functions, as Bartram and Bayliss (1984) point out: (a) select which test to administer; (b) present the testee with the necessary instruction; (c) administer the test; (d) record the test data; (e) analyse the results; (f) on the basis of this analysis, decide which test, if any, to administer next; (g) and finally produce an 'expert' interpretation of the results. No such system currently exists, although work is ongoing on all of the above functions. For this reason it is more accurate to use the term *computer-assisted assessment*. Furthermore, this term is likely to lead to greater acceptance of such systems by potential users insofar as it emphasizes the fact that the computer is being used to assist in the assessment of a client and not to completely replace the tester. Despite claims to the contrary, it seems likely that no completely automated testing system of the kind discussed by Bartram and Bayliss will appear for a few years yet. For convenience, however, the term *computerization* will be used in the remainder of this section without implying *complete automation*.

As far back as the early 1950s, accounting machines were being used to score automatically tests such as the *Minnesota Multiphasic Personality Inventory (MMPI)*. Even today, many automated systems are available to score *MMPI*s but the more sophisticated modern systems also generate interpretations of the results (Hedlund and Vieweg, 1988; Moreland, 1985, 1987). Interest in using computers to administer tests dates back to the late 1960s, when systems were developed using either time-sharing terminals attached to large mainframe computers or special purpose automated devices. Such systems were very expensive, inflexible and limited in their availability. Now that many professionals have ready access to powerful and inexpensive personal computers the use of computer-assisted assessment is increasing dramatically and looks set to do so for some time to come. Unfortunately, however, there is a feeling that new developments are often driven more by technological advances than by a coherent strategy that takes into account the likely impact of these developments on professional practice.

Before presenting an overview, references will be provided to a number of reviews of the area. The last ten years have seen a great increase in the number of publications in this field and a consequent increase in the appreciation of the issues raised. Limitations of space preclude an in-depth review, but the interested reader is referred to more detailed discussions by

Bartram and Bayliss (1984), Burke and Normand (1987), Butcher et al., (1985), French (1986), Hedlund and Vieweg (1988), Irvine et al. (in press), Sampson (1983, 1986a), Skinner and Pakula (1986), Taylor (1983) and Thompson, and Wilson (1982). Several journals have devoted special issues to computer-assisted assessment (see, for instance, Butcher, 1985; Sampson, 1986b; Wilpert, 1987). An extremely useful *Directory of Research into Automated Testing (DRAT)* is produced and regularly updated by Wilson (for example, Wilson, 1987).

The remainder of this section will deal with the advantages, both actual and potential, of computer-assisted assessment compared to more traditional testing methods. Consideration will also be given to potential problems in the use of computerized testing. Advice will be given to potential users and likely future trends will be outlined.

Advantages and Disadvantages

In principle, tests of all kinds may be computerized to some extent. In practice, given the limitations of current technology and software, certain types of test are much more amenable to computerization than others. For example, many tests of intelligence, aptitude, personality or interest involve the presentation of simple statements to which the testee must respond by selecting one from a choice of possible responses. Such tests may be adapted readily for computer presentation and scoring. Textual items are simply presented on the computer monitor and the testee responds by pressing the appropriate key via a standard keyboard or specialized keypad for example. The computer ensures standardization of presentation and speed and accuracy of scoring.

On the other hand, tests requiring open-ended responses such as those requiring natural language cannot be computerized until research in the field of artificial intelligence has advanced to the stage at which computers are able in some sense to understand natural language. This goal is not likely to be achieved for many years, perhaps decades, to come. In other areas, of course, the use of computers allows the testing of aptitudes and abilities which would be difficult to test in other ways. A good example is the MICROPAT system developed by Bartram (1987) for the selection of pilots, which includes tests of visuo-motor tracking and information management.

The actual question of which tests to automate has been determined as much by the type of hardware and software available as by any other consideration. Despite this, many types of tests have been automated to some extent. A good example of this variety is provided by the Leicester/DHSS project, a large-scale validation study of a number of computer-based tests involving several clinical sites in the UK (Beaumont and French, 1987). This study involved a verbal IQ test (the *Mill Hill Vocabulary Scale* [Synonyms]), a nonverbal IQ test (*Raven's Standard Progressive Matrices*), a personality test (*Eysenck Personality Questionnaire*), a neuropsychological test (*Wisconsin Card Sorting Test*), a test of directional sense (*The Money Standardized Test of Direction Sense*), a digit span procedure, and two aptitude tests (the *Language Usage* and *Spelling* subtests of the *Differential Aptitude Test Battery*). With respect to test batteries, it is often the case that although computer-based versions of some subtests can be produced relatively eas-ily, many present insurmountable problems given current technology.

Computer-assisted testing offers many advantages over traditional testing procedures, not least considerable potential savings in work-hours. When one considers the amount of time spent in training assessors and in actual test administration it is obvious that a completely automated system could pay for itself over a few months. In practice, however, few professionals are willing to allow completely unsupervised computer-based assessment al-though they may be willing to delegate the task to support staff.

Even the instructional phase of test presentation can be improved if the computer is used appropriately. Although traditional psychometric tests should always be administered in a standard way according to the direc-tions of the test manual, in practice human administrators are likely to vary considerably in the degree to which they actually follow these directions. Even fairly subtle differences in nonverbal communication during test ad-ministration could lead to differences in performance on the part of the testee. The computer will administer a test in a standardized manner at all times and this applies to all phases of testing, including the instructional phase.

Furthermore, the computer can assess the testee's understanding during the instructional phase and can be programmed to provide additional ex-planation of what is required if necessary. The computer will never lose pa-tience, but can politely terminate a session if it is apparent that the testee simply cannot understand how to complete the test. To date, few tests have taken advantage of the computer's flexibility during the instructional phase, mainly because most examples of computer-assisted assessment in-volve the adaptation of pre-existing tests and the emphasis has been on making the two versions as similar as possible. Hopefully this will change with the development of newer more sophisticated systems. It is essential that such instructions be developed and refined through empirical testing.

Computers can score responses and analyse results far more quickly and accurately than a person particularly if the test consists of many items or in-volves a complex scoring procedure (for example, MMPI). It is quite prob-able that many psychometrically valid tests have not found their way into general use precisely because they were complicated to administer, score and analyse in their traditional form. Such tests might be used much more widely if produced in computer-assisted form. Computers can also be used to generate interpretive reports for such tests as the MMPI. Moreland (1985) reviews this area and discusses the problems in validating such sys-tems.

Turning to a consideration of response input, the standard QWERTY keyboard is likely to remain the usual input device in computer-assisted as-sessment for some time to come despite its considerable ergonomic disad-vantages. Specialized keyboards often make life considerably easier for the testee and a standard keyboard for use in psychometric testing would be of great value.

Of course a variety of other input devices are available but it is essential that each is empirically evaluated for each application for which it is con-sidered. It must not be simply assumed that response input mode will have no effect on norms and reliability. The various input devices include touch screens, light pens, touch pads, bit pads, joysticks, tracker balls, mice, and speech recognition devices. In certain cases, computer-assisted assessment using specialized input devices can allow the testing of physically disabled people who would otherwise be untestable (Wilson and McMillan, 1986). Tests of visuomotor skill are likely to require analog input devices such as joysticks.

Although many automated systems require simple 'true/false', 'yes/no', or other multiple-choice responses, the computer does allow the collection of much more complex data such as reaction times. Furthermore, the computer can monitor the pattern of responses for so-called stereotyped responding which may indicate that the testee is not taking the test seriously, such as replying 'yes' to all odd-numbered items and 'no' to all even-numbered items (Huba, 1987).

Matarazzo (1983) has expressed concern that automation of tests might lead to the tests being used, or rather misused, on a much wider scale than is presently the case. This could follow from the fact that computer-assisted versions of tests are obviously designed in such a way that test administration requires only minimal training, if any. It is certainly the case that the number of commercially available programs passing themselves off as 'psychological tests' is on the increase allowing the home-computer user to 'assess' anything from personality and intelligence to psychic abilities. Sadly, of course, these products have usually not undergone anything resembling proper standardization procedures. As Matarazzo points out, the danger may be compounded by the fact that the tests have a spurious appearance of objectivity and infallibility as a halo effect from the computer.

While the danger of misuse of unstandardized tests by unqualified persons is one concern, paradoxically there has been a general resistance to the use of superior products by qualified potential users in the UK. (In North America, much more use is made of computer-based assessment.) This resistance may well be a reaction to claims made by system developers that testing can henceforth be left in the hands of support staff leaving the skilled professionals free to make better use of their skills. Such claims emphasize the routine unskilled aspects of testing. On the other hand, professionals involved in assessment have always claimed that it requires skills attained after much training. These professionals are referring to the more complex aspects of assessment such as test interpretation and guidance. Skilled and unskilled aspects can be separated. Blanket terms like 'computerized testing' cover all aspects of assessment from simple presentation of items and scoring of responses to the hypothetical completely automated assessment system. Close consultation between system developers and potential users is essential to clarify the degree to which the latter need to be or wish to be involved in the testing procedure.

It was originally feared that automated testing would be 'dehumanizing' and that clients would feel very negative about being tested in this way. In fact, a number of studies have shown that generally subjects respond as well to computer-based assessment as to human-administered tests, although there are a few exceptions to this generalization. French and Beaumont (1987) compared the reaction of psychiatric patients to standard and computer-based versions of a variety of tests. In general, both versions of the tests were evaluated positively and few differences were detected.

Where differences were found, the computer-based tests were rated as more enjoyable, especially in the case of the simpler tests, but were also rated as less clear and less comprehensible in the case of the more complex tests.

Advice to Users

The potential user does require at least a working knowledge of psychometrics to avoid the possibility of test misuse, as emphasized above. If one has such expertise, one needs an appropriate system in terms of hardware. Although it would be impossible, and indeed inappropriate, to provide firm guidelines on the hardware requirements for the use of computer-based assessment software, Bartram et al. (1987) suggest that the following minimum configuration would be appropriate: (a) full IBM-compatibility; (b) 256K RAM; (c) 10 Mbyte hard disk with single 360K drives; (d) colourgraphics adaptor with standard-resolution colour monitor; (e) one serial port and one parallel printer port; (f) 80-column dot matrix printer. Especially in the educational and clinical fields, however, the need to cater for the widespread use of BBC microcomputers is recognized. It is, of course, essential to ensure that any particular software package one wishes to use will actually run on one's system.

Bartram et al. provide recommendations for the design of software for computer-based assessment. The degree to which these recommendations have been followed provide the user with a means of evaluating software prior to use. Great attention must be paid to the quality of human–computer interaction. Specific recommendations are provided relating to, '(a) general information presentation; (b) screen layout; (c) information entry; (d) menu design; (e) form-filling; (f) spreadsheet design; (g) layout and presentation of test items' (p. 3). Adequate documentation of the software should always be provided.

It is most important that assessment software is well-designed and easy to use. Software should be 'crash-proof' and therefore appropriate checks should have been programmed into the system wherever necessary (including checks on hardware configuration prior to starting a session, data-entry checks throughout the session, and so on). The system should suggest appropriate remedial action if possible (for example, 'Please close disk drive door'). Only in this way will good rapport be achieved.

A major requirement in the production of computer-based versions of existing tests is to ensure that the computer-based test and the traditional test are psychometrically equivalent (see, for example, Standing Committee on Test Standards, 1984; French, 1985). Bartram et al. discuss this issue in detail. The user must always be aware of the quality of the standardization data available for a particular computerized test under consideration. If no documentation is available relating to this issue, the user cannot assume that the test is actually psychometrically valid. The usual approach in the past has been to assess test–retest and inter-mode reliability between the standard and a computer version of a test. Where appropriate the validity of the computer version may also be assessed. Even these steps will not ensure that the same norms can be used for the computer version as for the standard version. Bartram et al. recommend that a complete test–retest design should be employed covering all of the following combinations of versions: computer–computer, computer–traditional, traditional–computer, and traditional–traditional. They conclude, 'All automated versions of tests should be distributed with a supplement to the standard test manual which not only describes how to use the software but also presents the results of inter-mode equivalence studies. Where complete restandardization has not been carried out prior to publication, the confidence with which existing norms can be used should be clearly stated' (p. 32).

It is also often assumed that standardization of a computer-based test need only be carried out for one machine and that results can be safely generalized to other machines. Such intra-mode equivalence simply cannot be assumed for a variety of reasons, such as differences in item layout due to differences between machines in terms of textual or graphical resolution. Differences in response mode including such mundane factors as the layout of the numeric keys on the keyboard may also have an effect on norms. Each new version must be properly standardized.

In general, items will be presented on the computer monitor. Bartram et al. provide detailed recommendations relating to good screen layout. For example, use of highlighting, colour or underlining should be minimized and flashing text should be avoided altogether. Although such gimmicks may catch the eye, they can be confusing to testees and quickly become irritating. Clarity is paramount. If items consist of text only, then items usually transfer easily to the computer. With graphical items, however, problems can arise due to the limited resolution of computer graphics (see, for instance, Beaumont and French, 1987). Simple graphics can be presented on systems with a resolution of around 256 by 256 pixels, but 1024 by 1024 is essential for complex graphics.

Sound should also be used with discretion. If group testing is to be carried out sound-effects or tunes from neighbouring systems can be distracting and annoying. A case can probably be made for the limited use of such gimmicks when testing children individually, particularly if the test would otherwise be unduly tedious.

Finally, the implications of copyright laws must be taken into account. As summarized by Bartram et al., this means that:

> a) any software acquired commercially either under licence or as an outright purchase is the intellectual property of either the licensor or the author and may not be reproduced in any form without permission; b) any assessment instrument originally published in printed form may not be reproduced in whole or in part within any computer software without permission. This applies to any aspect of the assessment instrument and not just, for example, to the test items (p. 32).

Second, any procedure which involves the storage of personal information relating to identifiable individuals on a computer will come under the Data Protection Act (1984). Virtually all users of computer-based assessment systems in the UK therefore must register under the Act. The Act refers not only to long-term storage of such data but also to the collection and processing during a testing session. The reader is referred to The Data Protection Act, 1984, Guideline Number 1 (1985) for further details.

Future Trends

As stated, most work to date has concentrated on the adaptation of pre-existing tests. One particular possibility which the computer has raised is that of *adaptive* or *tailored testing*. Simply put, the idea is that on many tests one is able to predict how a testee would respond to a particular item on the basis of the responses to other items. For example, many IQ tests begin with simple items, well within the grasp of most of the population the test is aimed at, and gradually progress to difficult items beyond the ability of most testees. One can be fairly sure that if an individual can answer the hardest item correctly they could answer the simplest correctly, whether or not one actually administers it. Computers can be programmed to present just those items that are most appropriate for a particular individual and to infer the likely responses on the remaining items. Such programs can produce very similar estimates of ability to full versions of the tests while reducing testing time by more than half. It is likely that tailored testing will become much more common in the future.

Advances in technology will also be incorporated into future systems although the danger of using the technology for its own sake cannot be overemphasized. However, the use of interactive video and speech input/output technology raises interesting and exciting possibilities (French, 1986).

The development of totally new tests utilizing the full potential of the microcomputer is undoubtedly the most important challenge facing system developers today. The problem, of course, is that proper standardization is an expensive and time-consuming exercise especially for computer-based tests. It is a challenge, however, that must be faced. The merging of approaches from experimental cognitive psychology and psychometrics should prove to be extremely fruitful. Tests have been developed in which new items are generated according to pre-specified rules and which therefore present each testee with a new set of items. Such approaches have obvious advantages.

It is increasingly recognized that the next generation of computer-based assessment systems must be more 'intelligent' than the systems developed so far. Such testing systems must make use of the principles employed in other intelligent knowledge-based systems (IKBS) or so-called 'expert systems' to a much greater extent than they do at present. The ultimate aim will be to build up a picture of the test-taker's pattern of abilities, aptitudes, preferences, and so on, and perhaps to assess suitability for specific jobs and to offer vocational guidance and even training. It is crucial that such potential developments be considered in a wide social context.

References

BARTRAM, D. & BAYLISS, R. (1984). Automated testing: Past, present and future. *Journal of Occupational Psychology, 57*, 221–237.

BARTRAM, D. (1987). The development of an automated testing system for pilot selection: The MICROPAT project. *Applied Psychology: An International Review, 36*, 279–298.

BARTRAM, D., BEAUMONT, J.G., CORNFORD, T., DANN, P.L., & WILSON, S.L. (1987). Recommendations for the design of software for computer based assessment. Available from The British Psychological Society, St Andrew's House, 48 Princess Road East, Leicester LE1 7DR.

BEAUMONT, J.G. & FRENCH, C.C. (1987). A clinical field study of eight automated psychometric procedures: the Leicester/DHSS project. *International Journal of Man–Machine Studies, 26,* 661–682.

BURKE, M.J. & NORMAND, J. (1987). Computerized psychological testing: Overview and critique. *Professional Psychology: Research and Practice, 18,* 4–51.

BUTCHER, J.N. (Ed.) (1985). Computerized assessment [Special series]. *Journal of Consulting and Clinical Psychology, 53*(6).

BUTCHER, J.N., KELLER, L.S. & BACON, S.F. (1985). Current developments and future directions in computerized personality assessment. *Journal of Consulting and Clinical Psychology, 53,* 803–815.

FRENCH, C.C. (1985). Automated testing: The need for caution. *Guidance and Assessment Review, 2,* 5–6.

FRENCH, C.C. (1986). Microcomputers and psychometric assessment. *British Journal of Guidance and Counselling, 14,* 33–45.

FRENCH, C.C. & BEAUMONT, J.G. (1987). The reaction of psychiatric patients to computerized assessment. *British Journal of Clinical Psychology, 26,* 267–278.

HEDLUND, J.L. & VIEWEG, B.W. (1988). Automation in psychological testing. *Psychiatric Annals, 18,* 217–227.

HUBA, G.J. (1987). On probabilistic computer-based test interpretations and other expert systems. *Applied Psychology: An International Review, 36,* 357–373.

IRVINE, S.H., NEWSTEAD, S. & DANN, P. (Eds.) (in press). *Computer-based Human Assessment.* London: Nijhoff.

MATARAZZO, J.D. (1983). Computerized psychological testing [editorial]. *Science, 221,* 323.

MORELAND, K.L. (1985). Validation of computer-based test interpretations: Problems and prospects. *Journal of Consulting and Clinical Psychology, 53,* 816–825.

MORELAND, K.L. (1987). Computer-based test interpretations: Advice to the consumer. *Applied Psychology: An International Review, 36,* 385–399.

SAMPSON, J.P. (1983). Computer-assisted testing and assessment: Current status and implications for the future. *Measurement and Evaluation in Guidance, 15,* 293–299.

SAMPSON, J.P. (1986a). Computer technology and counselling psychology: Regression toward the machine? *Counselling Psychologist, 14,* 567–586.

SAMPSON, J.P. (Ed.) (1986b). Computer-assisted testing and assessment [Special issue]. *Measurement and Evaluation in Counselling and Development, 19*(1).

SKINNER, H.A. & PAKULA, A. (1986). Challenge of computers in psychological assessment. *Professional Psychology: Research and Practice, 17,* 44–50.

STANDING COMMITTEE ON TEST STANDARDS. (1984). Note on the computerization of printed psychological tests and questionnaires. *Bulletin of the British Psychological Society, 37,* 416–417.

TAYLOR, T.R. (1983). Computerized testing. *South African Journal of Psychology, 13,* 23–31.

The Data Protection Act, 1984, Guideline Number 1p An Introduction and Guide to the Act. (1985) Wilmslow: Office of the Data Protection Registrar.

THOMPSON, J.A. & WILSON, S.L. (1982). Automated psychological testing. *International Journal of Man–Machine Studies, 17,* 279–289.

WILPERT, B. (Ed.) (1987). Computerised psychological testing [Special issue]. *Applied Psychology: An International Review, 36*(3 & 4).

WILSON, S.L. (1987). *Directory of Research into Automated (Psychological and Psychiatric) Testing (DRAT).* Available from Dr Sarah L. Wilson, Research Department, The Royal Hospital & Home, West Hill, Putney, London, SW15 3SW.

WILSON, S.L. & McMILLAN, T.M. (1986). Finding able minds in disabled bodies. *The Lancet,* December 20/27, 1444–1446.

Appendix

Conversion of areas under the normal curve to Z and T scores

Area less than Z	Area from Mean to Z	Z-score	T-score
0.005	0.495	−2.5703	24
0.010	0.490	−2.3242	27
0.015	0.485	−2.1704	28
0.020	0.480	−2.0542	29
0.025	0.475	−1.9585	30
0.030	0.470	−1.8799	31
0.035	0.465	−1.8115	32
0.040	0.460	−1.7500	33
0.045	0.455	−1.6953	33
0.050	0.450	−1.6440	34
0.055	0.445	−1.5979	34
0.060	0.440	−1.5552	34
0.065	0.435	−1.5142	35
0.070	0.430	−1.4757	35
0.075	0.425	−1.4390	36
0.080	0.420	−1.4048	36
0.085	0.415	−1.3723	36
0.090	0.410	−1.3407	37
0.095	0.405	−1.3108	37
0.100	0.400	−1.2817	37
0.105	0.395	−1.2535	37
0.110	0.390	−1.2271	38
0.115	0.385	−1.2006	38
0.120	0.380	−1.1749	38
0.125	0.375	−1.1501	38
0.130	0.370	−1.1262	39
0.135	0.365	−1.1031	39
0.140	0.360	−1.0801	39
0.145	0.355	−1.0579	39
0.150	0.350	−1.0365	40
0.155	0.345	−1.0151	40
0.160	0.340	−0.9946	40
0.165	0.335	−0.9741	40
0.170	0.330	−0.9545	40
0.175	0.325	−0.9348	41
0.180	0.320	−0.9152	41
0.185	0.315	−0.8964	41
0.190	0.310	−0.8776	41
0.195	0.305	−0.8596	41

Area less than Z	Area from Mean to Z	Z-score	T-score
0.200	0.300	−0.8417	42
0.205	0.295	−0.8237	42
0.210	0.290	−0.8066	42
0.215	0.285	−0.7891	42
0.220	0.280	−0.7725	42
0.225	0.275	−0.7554	42
0.230	0.270	−0.7391	43
0.235	0.265	−0.7225	43
0.240	0.260	−0.7062	43
0.245	0.255	−0.6904	43
0.250	0.250	−0.6742	43
0.255	0.245	−0.6588	43
0.260	0.240	−0.6434	44
0.265	0.235	−0.6281	44
0.270	0.230	−0.6127	44
0.275	0.225	−0.5977	44
0.280	0.220	−0.5828	44
0.285	0.215	−0.5682	44
0.290	0.210	−0.5533	44
0.295	0.205	−0.5388	45
0.300	0.200	−0.5247	45
0.305	0.195	−0.5101	45
0.310	0.190	−0.4956	45
0.315	0.185	−0.4819	45
0.320	0.180	−0.4678	45
0.325	0.175	−0.4537	45
0.330	0.170	−0.4401	46
0.335	0.165	−0.4264	46
0.340	0.160	−0.4127	46
0.345	0.155	−0.3990	46
0.350	0.150	−0.3854	46
0.355	0.145	−0.3717	46
0.360	0.140	−0.3585	46
0.365	0.135	−0.3452	47
0.370	0.130	−0.3320	47
0.375	0.125	−0.3187	47
0.380	0.120	−0.3055	47
0.385	0.115	−0.2922	47
0.390	0.110	−0.2794	47
0.395	0.105	−0.2662	47
0.400	0.100	−0.2534	47
0.405	0.095	−0.2405	48
0.410	0.090	−0.2273	48
0.415	0.085	−0.2145	48
0.420	0.080	−0.2017	48
0.425	0.075	−0.1893	48
0.430	0.070	−0.1765	48
0.435	0.065	−0.1636	48
0.440	0.060	−0.1508	48

Area less than Z	Area from Mean to Z	Z-score	T-score
0.445	0.055	−0.1384	49
0.450	0.050	−0.1256	49
0.455	0.045	−0.1128	49
0.460	0.040	−0.1004	49
0.465	0.035	−0.0880	49
0.470	0.030	−0.0752	49
0.475	0.025	−0.0628	49
0.480	0.020	−0.0500	50
0.485	0.015	−0.0376	50
0.490	0.010	−0.0252	50
0.495	0.005	−0.0124	50
0.500	0.000	0.0000	50
0.505	0.005	0.0124	50
0.510	0.010	0.0252	50
0.515	0.015	0.0376	50
0.520	0.020	0.0500	50
0.525	0.025	0.0628	51
0.530	0.030	0.0752	51
0.535	0.035	0.0880	51
0.540	0.040	0.1004	51
0.545	0.045	0.1128	51
0.550	0.050	0.1256	51
0.555	0.055	0.1384	51
0.560	0.060	0.1508	52
0.565	0.065	0.1636	52
0.570	0.070	0.1765	52
0.575	0.075	0.1893	52
0.580	0.080	0.2017	52
0.585	0.085	0.2145	52
0.590	0.090	0.2273	52
0.595	0.095	0.2405	52
0.600	0.100	0.2534	53
0.605	0.105	0.2662	53
0.610	0.110	0.2794	53
0.615	0.115	0.2922	53
0.620	0.120	0.3055	53
0.625	0.125	0.3187	53
0.630	0.130	0.3320	53
0.635	0.135	0.3452	53
0.640	0.140	0.3585	54
0.645	0.145	0.3717	54
0.650	0.150	0.3854	54
0.655	0.155	0.3990	54
0.660	0.160	0.4127	54
0.665	0.165	0.4264	54
0.670	0.170	0.4401	54
0.675	0.175	0.4537	55
0.680	0.180	0.4678	55
0.685	0.185	0.4819	55

Area less than Z	Area from Mean to Z	Z-score	T-score
0.690	0.190	0.4956	55
0.695	0.195	0.5101	55
0.700	0.200	0.5247	55
0.705	0.205	0.5388	55
0.710	0.210	0.5533	56
0.715	0.215	0.5682	56
0.720	0.220	0.5828	56
0.725	0.225	0.5977	56
0.730	0.230	0.6127	56
0.735	0.235	0.6281	56
0.740	0.240	0.6434	56
0.745	0.245	0.6588	57
0.750	0.250	0.6742	57
0.755	0.255	0.6904	57
0.760	0.260	0.7062	57
0.765	0.265	0.7225	57
0.770	0.270	0.7391	57
0.775	0.275	0.7554	58
0.780	0.280	0.7725	58
0.785	0.285	0.7891	58
0.790	0.290	0.8066	58
0.795	0.295	0.8237	58
0.800	0.300	0.8417	58
0.805	0.305	0.8596	59
0.810	0.310	0.8776	59
0.815	0.315	0.8964	59
0.820	0.320	0.9152	59
0.825	0.325	0.9348	59
0.830	0.330	0.9545	60
0.835	0.335	0.9741	60
0.840	0.340	0.9946	60
0.845	0.345	1.0151	60
0.850	0.350	1.0365	60
0.855	0.355	1.0579	61
0.860	0.360	1.0801	61
0.865	0.365	1.1031	61
0.870	0.370	1.1262	61
0.875	0.375	1.1501	62
0.880	0.380	1.1749	62
0.885	0.385	1.2006	62
0.890	0.390	1.2271	62
0.895	0.395	1.2535	63
0.900	0.400	1.2817	63
0.905	0.405	1.3108	63
0.910	0.410	1.3407	63
0.915	0.415	1.3723	64
0.920	0.420	1.4048	64
0.925	0.425	1.4390	64
0.930	0.430	1.4757	65

Area less than Z	Area from Mean to Z	Z-score	T-score
0.935	0.435	1.5142	65
0.940	0.440	1.5552	66
0.945	0.445	1.5979	66
0.950	0.450	1.6440	66
0.955	0.455	1.6953	67
0.960	0.460	1.7500	68
0.965	0.465	1.8115	68
0.970	0.470	1.8799	69
0.975	0.475	1.9585	70
0.980	0.480	2.0542	71
0.985	0.485	2.1704	72
0.990	0.490	2.3242	73
0.995	0.495	2.5703	76

Conversion of Z-scores to areas under the normal curve

Z-score	Area from Z to mean	Area above Z	Area below Z
−3.5	0.4998	0.9998	0.0002
−3.4	0.4997	0.9997	0.0003
−3.3	0.4995	0.9995	0.0005
−3.2	0.4993	0.9993	0.0007
−3.1	0.4990	0.9990	0.0010
−3.0	0.4987	0.9987	0.0013
−2.9	0.4981	0.9981	0.0019
−2.8	0.4974	0.9974	0.0026
−2.7	0.4965	0.9965	0.0035
−2.6	0.4953	0.9953	0.0047
−2.5	0.4938	0.9938	0.0062
−2.4	0.4918	0.9918	0.0082
−2.3	0.4893	0.9893	0.0107
−2.2	0.4861	0.9861	0.0139
−2.1	0.4821	0.9821	0.0179
−2.0	0.4772	0.9772	0.0228
−1.9	0.4713	0.9713	0.0287
−1.8	0.4641	0.9641	0.0359
−1.7	0.4554	0.9554	0.0446
−1.6	0.4452	0.9452	0.0548
−1.5	0.4332	0.9332	0.0668
−1.4	0.4192	0.9192	0.0808
−1.3	0.4032	0.9032	0.0968
−1.2	0.3849	0.8849	0.1151
−1.1	0.3643	0.8643	0.1357
−1.0	0.3413	0.8413	0.1587
−0.9	0.3159	0.8159	0.1841
−0.8	0.2881	0.7881	0.2119
−0.7	0.2580	0.7580	0.2420
−0.6	0.2257	0.7257	0.2743

Z-score	Area from Z to mean	Area above Z	Area below Z
−0.5	0.1915	0.6915	0.3085
−0.4	0.1554	0.6554	0.3446
−0.3	0.1179	0.6179	0.3821
−0.2	0.0793	0.5793	0.4207
−0.1	0.0398	0.5398	0.4602
0.0	0.0000	0.5000	0.5000
0.1	0.0398	0.4602	0.5398
0.2	0.0793	0.4207	0.5793
0.3	0.1179	0.3821	0.6179
0.4	0.1554	0.3446	0.6554
0.5	0.1915	0.3085	0.6915
0.6	0.2257	0.2743	0.7257
0.7	0.2580	0.2420	0.7580
0.8	0.2881	0.2119	0.7881
0.9	0.3159	0.1841	0.8159
1.0	0.3413	0.1587	0.8413
1.1	0.3643	0.1357	0.8643
1.2	0.3849	0.1151	0.8849
1.3	0.4032	0.0968	0.9032
1.4	0.4192	0.0808	0.9192
1.5	0.4332	0.0668	0.9332
1.6	0.4452	0.0548	0.9452
1.7	0.4554	0.0446	0.9554
1.8	0.4641	0.0359	0.9641
1.9	0.4713	0.0287	0.9713
2.0	0.4772	0.0228	0.9772
2.1	0.4821	0.0179	0.9821
2.2	0.4861	0.0139	0.9861
2.3	0.4893	0.0107	0.9893
2.4	0.4918	0.0082	0.9918
2.5	0.4938	0.0062	0.9938
2.6	0.4953	0.0047	0.9953
2.7	0.4965	0.0035	0.9965
2.8	0.4974	0.0026	0.9974
2.9	0.4981	0.0019	0.9981
3.0	0.4987	0.0013	0.9987
3.1	0.4990	0.0010	0.9990
3.2	0.4993	0.0007	0.9993
3.3	0.4995	0.0005	0.9995
3.4	0.4997	0.0003	0.9997
3.5	0.4998	0.0002	0.9998

Significance of Correlation Coefficients

If the number of people = N, then the degrees of freedom (df) for the correlation are (N–2). If the relevant df is not given in the table, use the next smaller value. Correlations larger than the appropriate tabled value are significantly greater than r = 0.0 at the stated level of significance. In general it is safest to use the 2-tail values wherever either a positive or negative correlation could arise. For other cases (for example, test–retest measures) where negative values would not make sense, use 1-tail tests.

df	p=0.05 (2-tail) p=0.025 (1-tail)	df	p=0.05 (2-tail) p=0.025 (1-tail)
5	0.754	34	0.329
6	0.707	36	0.320
7	0.666	38	0.312
8	0.632	40	0.304
9	0.602	42	0.297
10	0.576	44	0.291
11	0.553	46	0.284
12	0.532	48	0.279
13	0.514	50	0.273
14	0.497	55	0.261
15	0.482	60	0.250
16	0.468	65	0.241
17	0.456	70	0.232
18	0.444	75	0.224
19	0.433	80	0.217
20	0.423	85	0.211
21	0.413	90	0.205
22	0.404	95	0.200
23	0.396	100	0.195
24	0.388	125	0.174
25	0.381	150	0.159
26	0.374	175	0.148
27	0.367	200	0.138
28	0.361	300	0.113
29	0.355	400	0.098
30	0.349	500	0.088
32	0.339	1000	0.062

Glossary

Alternate form reliability
The *reliability* of two or more correlated or equivalent forms of a test. (See also *coefficient of equivalence*.)

Bivariate distributions
Distributions of measures on two variables. For instance, the bivariate frequency distribution of age and height shows the relationship between the two variables. For a sample of scores this can be shown by a three-dimensional histogram (see Figure 2.4). In the case of a population the normal distribution would have a three-dimensional bell-shape.

Coefficient of consistency
This is a measure of *reliability*. It is the mean of the corrected correlations between all possible split halves. A simple way of calculating internal consistency is by means of Cronbach's alpha, which is based on the ratio of individual item or part variances to the overall scale score variance.

Coefficient of dependability
This is similar to the *coefficient of stability* except that it refers to the short-term measure (two weeks or less) from the test to retest to obtain the correlation coefficient.

Coefficient of equivalence
This is the *correlation coefficient* between Form A and Form B of a test given immediately after one another and when each form is designed to be equivalent to the other.

Coefficient of stability
First see *test–retest correlation*. Coefficient of stability is another name occasionally used for a *test–retest correlation* coefficient used as a reference to the partial dependence of the correlation on the stability over time of the trait being measured. It is useful to consider this in juxtaposition to the *coefficient of dependability*.

Construct validity
The construct validity of a test refers to whether the test is measuring what it is supposed to measure. This is a matter of judgement based on accumulated evidence.

Correlation
This roughly means, in statistical terms, the extent of the linear relationship between two or more variables. In other words, two variables are correlated when a systematic increase in the magnitude of one variable leads to a corresponding increase or decrease in the other.

Correlation coefficient
When calculated this is a number varying between 1.00, indicating a perfect positive correlation, and −1.00, indicating a perfect negative correlation. The relationship is positive when an increase in one variable produces a systematic increase in the other. Conversely the relationship is negative if one variable increases while the other decreases. A correlation of zero means that there is no linear relationship between the two variables.

Deductive validation
See *validation, deductive.*

Dependent variable
See *variable, dependent.*

Distribution, frequency
See *frequency distribution.*

Frequency distribution
This is the term for any distribution that lists the frequency of occurrence of scores according to categories or classes.

Histogram
A *frequency distribution* that is presented pictorially. The number of cases in each class is represented by a vertical bar.

Independent variable
See *variable, independent.*

Inductive validation
See *validation, deductive.*

Mean
In common parlance this is the average of a number of scores. That is, the sum of the scores divided by the number of scores, for example, the mean of 3, 4, 7 and 8 is $22/4 = 5.5$.

Median
This is calculated by arranging a set of scores in rank order and then choosing the middle score or taking the average of the middle two. The virtue of this measure over the mean is that extreme scores will not distort the median value. However, the mean score is used much more frequently, while the median is used only for distributions that are very skewed.

Mode
When a histogram is plotted of the distribution of a sample of scores on a variable, the score of the midpoint of the class interval of the most frequent score is treated as the mode. This measure is rarely used except when a distribution might have more than one mode. Furthermore it should only be used when there is a large number of scores available.

Multitrait, multimethod matrix (MTMM)
In its simplest form, two distinct constructs are defined, and two distinct methods for measuring each. The correlations between the four possible comparisons give information on the validity of the constructs.

Norm table
This is a table of values that is representative of a group or groups and which can be used as a means of comparing individuals.

Normal distribution
The normal distribution is critically important in statistical theory and consists of a mathematically specified distribution that is only approximated in nature. It is a hypothetical bell-shaped probability distribution and it is symmetrical with the *mean*, *mode* and *median* having the same value.

Population
A population is a set of individuals or measurements that have a common characteristic. It is perhaps best understood in the context of what constitutes a sample. A sample is a subset of the population. For example, subjects might be timed while naming each of a hundred pictures. The 100 pictures are a sample from an infinite population of possible pictures.

Raw scores
Having administered a test, the tester sums up the scores to derive the raw score of the testee on the test. At this point the raw scores have not been transformed. These raw scores are then usually converted either to percentile scores or to some form of *standard score*.

Regression
Suppose one plots the values of the *dependent variable*, Y, on the vertical axis against the *independent variable*, X, on the horizontal. A regression equation can be calculated on these scores so that for any value of X the value of Y can be predicted.

Reliability
This is a generic term for the dependability of a test. In other words, this is the extent to which a test gives consistent results from one occasion to the next on the same subject.

Standard deviation
A measure of the variability of a sample of scores from the average or mean of that same sample. It is often referred to as the SD. When the standard deviation is that of a population or sample, the Greek letter delta (δ) is employed. When it is used to estimate a population SD from a sample one, the letter S is used.

Standard score
This is a measure, such as the *z-score*, which is connected with the extent of the standard deviation.

Test–retest reliability
This is the *correlation* between two administrations of the same test to the same sample of subjects.

True score
When a person is measured they are hypothesized to have an amount of a characteristic. This amount is the true score, but as measuring involves error, to some degree, the obtained score will not normally be the same as the true score.

Univariate distributions
Frequency distributions of measures on a single variable.

Validity
This is the generic term for the extent of the meaningfulness and appropriateness of the conclusions made on the outcome of a test.

Validation, deductive
This assumes that we start with a theory in order that the content of the test is defined and that hypotheses are generated concerning what should correlate with the test scores. (See also *validation, inductive.*)

Validation, inductive
This starts with the test measure and then tries to infer what it must be a measure of by examining its relationship with other things.

Variable, dependent
Assuming a relationship between the dependent and *independent variable*, the values of the dependent variable are the result of changes in the values of the independent variable.

Variable, independent
A variable that is experimentally manipulated so that the effect on the *dependent variable(s) may be observed.*

Variation or dispersion
This is a generic term for the variability of individuals along various dimensions, such as height and intelligence. It is normally measured by means of the *standard deviation*. It also refers to the distribution of scores on variables. (See *normal distribution*.)

z-scores
The *standard score*, z, of a *raw score* X is the difference between X and the mean divided by the standard deviation. For example, suppose the score is 105, the mean of the sample from which the score comes is 102 and the standard deviation of the sample is 15; then the z-score will be $(105 - 102)/15$, which is 0.2. In this case the z-score is 0.2 standard deviations above the mean.

Subject Index

Author Index